P9-DFS-703

Writing
for
Animals

Writing for Animals

An anthology for writers and
instructors to educate and inspire

Ashland
Creek
Press

Flagstaff Public Library
Flagstaff, Arizona

Writing for Animals: An anthology for writers and instructors
to educate and inspire
Edited by John Yunker

Published by Ashland Creek Press
Ashland, Oregon
www.ashlandcreekpress.com

© 2018 Ashland Creek Press

All rights reserved. No part of this book may be reproduced
or transmitted, in any form or by any means, without written
permission of the publisher.

ISBN 978-1-61822-058-5
Library of Congress Control Number: 2018931653

The essay "No One Mourns an Unnamed Animal: Why
Naming Animals Might Help Save Them" first appeared in
the September 19, 2016, issue of *Zoomorphic Magazine*.

The essay "Giving Animals a Voice: Letters from an
Ashland Deer" first appeared in *Minding Nature*, Vol.
11, No. 2 (May 2018), a publication of the Center for
Humans and Nature (www.humansandnature.org). The
letters to the deer were originally published in the July 2015
and September 2015 issues of *Sneak Preview* magazine, and
the deer profile was published in the September 2016 issue.

Contents

Introduction

The more we study animals, the smarter they get.

Whales, we now know, communicate in complex languages over hundreds of miles; are curious, playful, and highly social; and can recognize themselves and others in a mirror. We know that sharks can sense how fast your heart is beating, and a polar bear can smell you from twenty miles away. Crows remember human faces, craft tools, and have long relied on the tires of passing cars as their personal nutcrackers. Bumble bees, like our companion animals, can be taught to pull strings and push balls in exchange for treats. Thanks to the efforts of professional and citizen scientists, we know so much more about animals than we knew just a generation ago.

Yet despite all we've learned, we have a long way to go when it comes to appreciating what animals can do. Because the skillset of a whale or a bumble bee doesn't position that animal for success in a hospital or on Wall Street, our society continues to view and treat nonhuman animals as lesser creatures.

Writers in all media, from fiction to film, bear some responsibility for our collective ignorance and mistreatment of animals. Nothing makes me cringe more in a story when I see animals used as mere props or set pieces: A man falls off a boat into the ocean, so cue the shark to elicit fear out of the reader, even though the fact is, sharks very rarely attack people. Bears and wolves all too often suffer the same fate: They are pulled into the story when the writer needs an easy way to crank up the tension.

Consider the long-term impact of so many writers treating so many animals similarly—a planet of people who do not shed tears when sharks have their fins removed or when wolves are killed to protect cattle (who themselves are slaughtered by the billions at the hands of humans). Other misconceptions commonly propagated by writers include: Pigs are messy, fish don't feel pain, horses enjoy running with humans on their backs. Even the words and phrases we use have a collective, subconscious impact: *pigsty, like a beached whale, kill two birds with one stone, don't be a chicken.* Through their work and their art, writers have the power to give animals a voice among humans—yet if we give animals a lesser voice or an inauthentic voice, we do animals a disservice.

For society to change its views, writers must change their views. We must look closely at how we depict animals and ask ourselves difficult questions. For example, are we using animals for our writing in a way that is authentic and fair? Or are we using them for our own purposes, leading to further misconceptions and abuses?

Animals have, both in literature and in life, been unfairly used by humans for millennia. Yet as our awareness awakens about animals' intelligence, sensitivity, and capacity for such "human" emotions as love, grief, and joy, literature, too, is reflecting this change in awareness. From Franz Kafka's *A Report to the Academy* to Karen Joy Fowler's *We*

Are All Completely Beside Ourselves, animals have played an increasingly central role in the literature of the last hundred years, and writers are contributing to this advancing awareness of animal issues through the written word, giving animals the voices they deserve.

Yet little has been written about the *process* of writing about animals—from crafting point of view to giving animals realistic voices. Writers face many questions and choices in their work, from how to educate without being didactic to how to develop animals as characters for an audience that still views them as ingredients.

Writing *for*, Not Merely *About*

When we chose the title of this collection, we deliberately chose *Writing* for *Animals* over *Writing* about *Animals*. While you will find much in this book to assist you in writing about animals, we wanted this book to go further, to help writers understand not only the process but the responsibility of writing about animals.

As writers, we live in an era in which animal suffering is becoming more evident to more people, while animals are under continuing threats through a possible next great extinction. And for those who do not yet see this or who choose not to see this, reading a realistic, accurate, and sensitively written story, poem, or novel about an animal can open hearts and minds to the reality of this suffering and loss.

Writing for Animals is designed for writers across genres, inviting them to take a closer look at how they treat animals in their work and offering examples and tips along the way. The book is organized into four parts, beginning with the writer as "naturalist." Like any scientifically trained naturalist, the writer faces profound and conflicting moral questions. For starters, Joanna Lilley asks if we have a right to write about animals and, if so, what responsibilities do all writers bear? And when documenting the suffering that so many animals endure at the hands of humans, she notes:

> It isn't easy writing about animals; it is complicated and complex, both intellectually and emotionally. Most of us, I suspect, do it because we must rather than as a conscious choice. When I stand for hours in galleries of extinct animals, sometimes I don't think I can do it anymore. But bearing witness gives me a place to stand and look, and a defendable reason for standing and looking.

Lisa Johnson, in "Animals that Work in Stories," explores some of the key roles that animals play in literature, covering authors such as Jack London and J.M. Coetzee. And in "The Case for More Reality in Writing *for* Animals," Rosemary Lombard makes a compelling argument, outlining a process that places animal characters on equal ground with their human counterparts.

> The process of learning to know the animals is similar to writing about our own species. The research is like doing historical research as a background for story, yet, in fiction, having the freedom to depart from it in some ways. Likewise, structuring animal characters is similar to structuring human characters, creating a suite of characteristics of body, place, and behavior, but realistic details are even more important because

of one huge, obvious difference: The animals, except a few in communication training, don't share our language. Their repertoire consists of gestures, vocalizations, scent, postures, eye/pupil change, and more; some of that we can learn. You can also use talking animals, put words in their thoughts, or have humans talk about them, but each of those choices also involves knowing the animals well, including details of appearance, place, and behavior.

In Part II, we dive into the craft of writing for animals. In "Meeting the Wild Things Where They Are," Kipp Wessel takes a holistic approach to the writing process, reminding us of our connections with animals:

> Animals, whether bounding through the backyard sumac or the Serengeti, are as dimensional as their human neighbors. Those of us who share our homes with them already know this truth. A dog is not a dog. A dog is. A barn owl is. An aardvark is. Animals are as sentient and multifaceted as any human being (sometimes more so). We need to be reminded of this when we delve into the writing of animal lives within the stories we tell. Regardless of nostrils or gills, those who have two feet or twenty, many vertebrae or none—each animal, bird, and reptile of the world has a life force and personality all its own.

In "Rewilding Literature," Paula MacKay shows how writers

can use creative nonfiction to foster empathy for wolves and other predators, inspiring compassion. She stresses that the first step in the process is rewilding oneself. She cites John Valliant, Ann Pancake, Peter Matthiessen and Aldo Leopold. She writes: "[I]t doesn't benefit predators to rob them of their wildness by taming the terms used to describe them (to call a grizzly bear *cuddly*, for instance) ... We must choose our words carefully when writing about wildlife and use language that helps move people toward a more empathetic point of view."

Hannah Sandoval provides a detailed character analysis of one of the more famous dogs in literature: Stephen King's Cujo in "Rabies Bites." And Beth Lyons tackles veganism and the fantasy genre with "Real Advocacy Within Fantasy Worlds."

Hunter Liguore, in "Writing Animals Where You Are," makes the case for focusing more on the animals you encounter every day:

> When writers are willing to meet animals where they live, the hierarchy of certain animals being more important can fall away. What's more, writers can start working *right now*, without the impediment of waiting until a "better animal" comes along.
>
> Last, and most important, we become solid witnesses to our world and can give voices to the animals we—and our readers—encounter more frequently. If I write about the mice in my attic, I might connect with someone who also has mice in the attic, or if I write about the groundhog that comes each season, I might share something and

connect with someone who also sees groundhogs. Not everyone sees lions, tigers, and bears every day. Together, though, we can work to give voice to the diversity of the animal kingdom.

In Part III, we tackle anthropomorphism. While scientists are taught not to project human qualities onto animals, writers can project anything they wish—but even writers are often cautioned against placing animals on equal footing with their human counterparts.

In "Other Nations," Marybeth Holleman discusses how one writes about an "other" species. She notes, "Writing about the nonhuman world is a practice in standing in the middle."

And in "No One Mourns an Unnamed Animal," Midge Raymond discusses the relationship between naming animals and empathy for animals.

> When we give an animal a name, we give it an identity, an individuality that sets it apart from the rest of its nameless species. And, in doing so, we often can't help but develop an emotional attachment to these named creatures.

The final part of the book is dedicated to inspiring writers to use their work to change the world. Writers have the unique ability not only to highlight the problems of today in ways that can reach the broadest of audiences but also to imagine a better, more compassionate tomorrow.

Sangamithra Iyer's essay asks "Are You Willing?" She writes, "Writing about animals in a way that challenges rather than accepts societal norms is a radical act. Any radical act is often met with resistance."

In "With a Hope to Change Things," Alex Lockwood interviews the founders of *Zoomorphic* magazine, an online and print journal with a clear point of view regarding the future of animal-centric writing.

Finally, we have assembled a resource list for writers that comprises journals, blogs, and magazines dedicated to publishing environmental and animal-centric fiction and nonfiction.

What is the role of the writer in this age, the Anthropocene? In a time when the world has been forever changed by humans, we can begin to change it for the better. The way humans treat nonhuman animals has significant impacts not only on our own psyches but on the planet itself.

We invite writers to imagine a world in which there is less suffering, more justice, purer water, cleaner air—and each of these things is connected, in some way, to the way we treat animals: for food, for entertainment, for resources. We invite writers to imagine our similarities with our nonhuman counterparts rather than our differences. And finally, we invite writers to use their talents to show these things to the world. I hope this book will help all writers do just that.

John Yunker
Ashland, Oregon
August 2018

Part I:
The Writer as
Naturalist

Do We Have the Right to Write about Animals?

Joanna Lilley

The girl took the poker her father handed her. As she looked up at him, he put his hand on her back and pushed her forward, closer to the animal crouching by a heap of rocks. Whatever the creature was, she'd never seen one before. It was the size of a large dog and had broad, dark stripes on its back and a wide face.

> "Go on," her father said. "It killed our sheep."
> The girl stood with her feet apart. She raised the poker with both hands.

I'm going to stop there because it's hard to write about the death of one of the last Tasmanian tigers ever to exist, particularly at the hands of a child, even if I am writing fiction. At least I hope I am. Reading *The Doomsday Book of Animals* by David Day, it isn't difficult to speculate that something like this may well have happened. Day writes that all the attacks on humans by Tasmanian tigers were made by animals who were "found to be starving and almost toothless, being easily killed or driven off by sticks or, in one case, a poker swung by a child."

I have feared the worst in my interpretation of those words and assumed that the poker was used to kill, not only drive off, the creature. I hope I am wrong.

We make many choices when we write. You may have noticed there are three potential points of view in the scene I've started here—the child's, the father's, and the Tasmanian tiger's—and I haven't opted for any of them yet. I, as the narrator, am not inside anyone's head. The scene so far describes no one's feelings. If I carried on writing the scene, I would have to commit to a point of view; I would need to show the reader what at least one of the characters is feeling, or avoiding feeling. Otherwise, unless I had great skill as a writer, the story would fall flat. The detached style would fail to draw in the reader.

The point of view I'd find most intriguing would be the tiger's. (Actually, the Tasmanian tiger wasn't a tiger at all but a marsupial, and I'll call it by one of its other names, thylacine, from now on.) But how can I possibly know what that particular thylacine was feeling? How can I know what any thylacine once felt? Did the very last thylacine that we're aware of, who died in a cage in Hobart Zoo in 1936 after being neglected by staff, know she was the only remaining example of her kind? I recognize that sounds fanciful, but we have very little idea what animals think and feel and perceive. This is the biggest challenge for writers trying to write authentically about animals. Do we have the ability, let alone the right, to presume what any creature is thinking or feeling?

I believe that, yes, we do have the ability and we do have the right to presume, conjecture, speculate, imagine, and explore what an animal might be experiencing. After all, we are animals, too. We forget this. Indeed, we are trained to believe we are not animals. This may not have been explicitly said to us during our *Homo sapiens* childhood (although the parental reprimand, "You're not an animal. Don't behave like one!" is not uncommon). The training tends to be more implicit, conveyed to us through attitudes and behaviors and through our cultural or religious influences.

Despite this training, perhaps we were confused when we observed that we lived with cats and dogs and rabbits and yet ate cows and chickens and pigs. Maybe the family dog was put down because the treatment for a tumor was expensive, and yet our grandmother lived her last years in a costly care home and didn't know who we were when we visited. Perhaps our parents criticized our uncle for caring more about his dog than about his nephews and nieces. Maybe our mother hit a rabbit on the highway and winced but carried on driving.

If we wish to write about animals, it is important to be aware of our influences and beliefs, chosen or imposed, evident or disguised, as this is the de facto training that has made us forget our own animal status. To help you, here are some questions you can ask yourself as a writer. You can also direct the same questions to your human and, yes, your animal characters.

Is an animal an "it" or a "he" or a "she" or a "they"?

Is an animal a "that" or a "who"?

In what circumstances could you kill an animal?

In what circumstances could you kill a Homo sapiens?

Do you believe humans have souls?
Do you believe animals have souls?

Our beliefs about animals can come from many different sources. Each of us is, of course, influenced by a unique set of circumstances including families, friends, economic status, class, education, religion, and geography.

For the past ten years, for example, I have lived in Yukon in Canada, next to Alaska. There are fourteen First Nations in Yukon, and the legends and stories passed on to them by their grandmothers teach them that Crow started the world:

> He brought fish to the lakes; he brought the first
> light into the world by letting the sun, moon and
> the stars escape from a wealthy man, who owned
> them. Crow placed these into the sky so they
> would belong to everyone.

The implication that Crow rescued the sun, moon, and stars from the tyranny of man appeals to me more than the depiction of creation we find in the Bible, yet I admit both versions of creation are just stories to me. What did your religion or culture teach you to believe about animals? Our beliefs can be contradictory and complicated. In Hinduism, cows are revered and never killed. The Nivkh people honored bears in festivals, then killed and ate them, and in Judaism, pigs are never eaten because they are considered unclean.

For my part, I grew up in England, a country that is ostensibly Christian, though my parents only took me and my siblings to church once a year, on Christmas Day. Christians believe God created animals for human beings and that we can therefore use them however we want. Christians believe animals are inferior to humans because they don't have souls and aren't capable of reason. I hope I have oversimplified the relationship of modern Christians to animals, but these statements feel true to the culture I grew up inside. Which is why, presumably, that culture finds it acceptable to keep billions of animals in extreme confinement and then kill and eat them.

What is notably confusing is that like millions of *Homo sapiens* of varying cultures, I assume, I was trained as a baby to listen to stories about animals and look at pictures of animals. It's astounding how many children's books are about our fellow creatures, albeit animals who can talk in human language and wear clothes and are invariably cute. Their reward for behaving like us is perhaps that the stories have happy endings. (It is interesting that when animals feature in adult stories, such as novels and films, they are highly likely to come to a sticky end. The humans might get a happy ending, but the animals rarely do.)

Like millions of other human children, I would persuade my parents to read me as many stories as possible and afterwards snuggle down to sleep among my stuffed toys—my monkey, bear, horse, and cat—and in the morning I would pour milk meant for baby cows on my cereal and at lunchtime eat a pig sandwich.

And so, when we write about animals, we need to know what belief system we are writing within and be aware of whether we are upholding, questioning, or opposing it. We must choose every word we use to describe an animal or convey an animal presence consciously, thoughtfully, deliberately. We must be able to explain each choice if we are called upon to do so. I mean, here, the words we select and what they create: vocabulary, diction, image, scene. (I am not saying the idea for a story or poem in itself can necessarily be conscious or deliberate. In my experience, an idea will simply come to us, and we will be compelled to write about it.)

Is, for example, the animal in your story or poem a metaphor for the natural or the true? (Your protagonist sees a grizzly bear on a hillside and wishes she were as free.) Is the animal there to show how cruel a human character is? (Your antagonist kicks a dog.) Do the animals have any agency of their own, or are they props in a scene? (A cat curled up by a fireside to denote domestic harmony.) Or a plot device? (If the child hadn't been running after a dog she wouldn't have been hit by a car.) Are they there as a comic turn? (Comedy isn't my strong point; perhaps a raccoon overturns a garbage can while a teenager is trying to sneak back into a house at night.)

Could you write a story or a poem that includes an animal that isn't serving a human purpose? Could you write about what the cat curled up by the fireside does when the husband and wife in the room start arguing?

Could you write a story or poem without any human beings in it at all?

When I started my current project of writing poems about extinct species, I wanted to be able to write poems that had no human presence in them and were not even filtered through a human experience. I wanted to be absent, for the animals to be able to communicate for themselves. I knew it was impossible, for writing is a human artifact, and I can't, unfortunately, experience anything unless it is through my own consciousness. Yet the fact that I have this urge is promising. If I'm thinking this way, then thousands of others will be, too. That's generally how it seems to work. Philosophers such as Peter Singer and his work on speciesism have propped the door open for people like me, and more and more of us are walking through. (As long ago as 2003, J.M. Coetzee's eponymous character, Elizabeth Costello, likened our treatment of animals to the treatment of humans in the Holocaust. Consider that.)

It is exciting that our minds are at least capable of attempting to experience a consciousness other than our own.

So, as animals ourselves, we are giving ourselves permission to write about other animals. Now, how do we go about knowing what those other animals are thinking or feeling? Here are some more questions for us to think about.

Have you ever lowered your hands and knees to the grass on a warm day and synchronized your breathing with the dog lying beside you? Have you ever opened your mouth when no one is looking and let your tongue loll? Have you been for a walk at night and, like the dog beside you, never looked up at the stars?

Have you slow-blinked at your cat when she looked at you? Have you lapped water with your tongue from a glass? Have you spent hours watching sparrows fly in and out of a hedge? Have you growled in your sleep? Perhaps you've purred.

Find an animal. In your house or garden, in the park or forest, on a mountain, in a zoo or on a safari, in a book or on YouTube. Find a cat, a dog. Find a wasp, ant, beetle, robin, raven, squirrel, gazelle, beaver, badger, fox, pheasant.

Watch that animal. Untighten your face, lower your shoulders, let your arms hang, feel from the inside every part of your body and relax each one: your muscles, your heart, your liver, your spine, the soles of your feet. Loosen your molecules; let them float apart. In this state, watch an animal.

Now let the space between you soften. Let the animal's form drift toward yours. Go closer to the other creature without physically moving. Feel as if you are merging. Let your skin slacken and become more permeable. Dissolve the air, paper, screen between you.

Become fur, chitin, bone, feather, fossil.

Pick up your pen. Touch the tips of your fingers to your keyboard. Write. Write sentences, if they happen to come, or just words. Make a row of marks and then another: your code for translating human experience.

This is not a technique that will appeal to every writer; it is just one way of attempting to connect with what another animal is thinking or feeling. We are skilled at doing this with our fellow human beings. I think we can get better at doing it with animals, too. I have shared this perhaps rather whimsical method with you because I find it to be an effective approach and also because it makes it clear that my own attitude toward animals is based on something we might call *intuition* or *emotion* rather than scientific study and analysis. Self-awareness is always useful. I have learned from years of writing that however much I want to be rational, scientific, factual, methodical, I write from a place of feeling. Almost all of what I am sharing here is what I know from personal experience rather than what I've learned through courses in animal studies (I haven't taken any) or from the writings of Jeremy Bentham, Peter Singer, Jane Goodall, Elisa Aaltola (read them if you can) and many others.

Nevertheless, observation, I believe, is the bridge between a subjective and an objective approach to writing about animals. I have observed the skull of a thylacine at the Royal Ontario Museum in Ontario, Canada. I have seen the extinct Xerces blue butterfly in a drawer in Regina, Canada. I have traveled three and a half thousand miles from my home in Whitehorse to meet Martha, the last-ever passenger pigeon, at the National Museum of Natural History in Washington, DC.

I speculated earlier, perhaps fancifully, whether the last thylacine in captivity knew she was potentially the last of her species. I have the same question, arguably more fittingly, for Martha, who died in 1914 at the Cincinnati Zoo. Perhaps my question is entirely anthropomorphic. Perhaps it is based on what I know to be true about passenger pigeons.

In 1866, a flock of passenger pigeons flew over Ontario in Canada. The flock was a mile wide and three hundred miles long. According to the Center for Biological Diversity, it took fourteen hours for them all to pass overhead. It's hard enough to imagine what it would have felt like to stand watching an ocean of birds flow above you, let alone what it would have been like to have been one of the birds themselves.

While I stood looking at Martha in Washington, DC, I wanted to know what it was like to be a small bird in a flock of millions. Complicating my efforts to empathize with Martha was the fact that I had read she was born in captivity. Were the two males displayed beside her born in captivity, too? What had it been like for Martha be confined in a cage at the zoo as she was now confined inside a glass case at the museum? I had so many questions for the small brown bird, yet all I could do was make notes, take photographs, and sketch, badly, her graceful shape.

The point is that passenger pigeons are said to have been one of the most social species of land birds. As human beings, we're used to being in large crowds—at a railway station, in a bar, at a concert—but is there something else going on when millions of individuals fly together as they migrate?

As a social animal, whether born in captivity or not, what would have been Martha's experience of solitude and confinement? Would she have had a sense of boredom? Or incompleteness? Did Martha attempt to connect or merge with other life she saw around her? Would the *Homo sapiens* visitors standing on the other side of the bars have provided an alternative social structure for her to attempt to become part of?

I wonder if my speculation about whether Martha knew she was the last of her species is so fanciful after all?

I have a final question for anyone who is trying to write about animals. Do we always know why we want to write about animals, why we have the urge to write from their point of view, express what they are thinking and feeling? We don't necessarily have to know, but I believe it's a worthwhile question to ask. I didn't used to be able to articulate why I felt compelled to write about animals. (I didn't even realize that animals featured in everything I wrote until it was pointed out to me by author Patrick Neate at an Arvon writing course.)

For the last year or so, however, I have had an answer. I only have it due to a conversation with a friend who is vegan and committed to helping animals. I was complaining about animal welfare organizations e-mailing me gruesome images of suffering animals, such as a monkey with electrodes in her head or a fox cut in two by a snare. I said they were preaching to the converted. I didn't need to see it; I already knew what went on.

My friend pointed out that she felt obligated to look at such images. Someone had to bear witness to animals' suffering, she said. We mustn't shirk from knowing how cruelly animals are being treated; we must not look away. Since that conversation, and a knowing in my navel that she was right, I have become more willing to bear witness. I recognize that it is the humans advocating for animals who are engineering the opportunity for me to bear witness. The animals themselves cannot present their suffering to me; I may or may not happen across it and mostly will not in my comfortable, Western life. That, I believe, was my friend's point.

It isn't easy writing about animals; it is complicated and complex, both intellectually and emotionally. Most of us, I suspect, do it because we must rather than as a conscious choice. When I stand for hours in galleries of extinct animals, sometimes I don't think I can do it anymore. But bearing witness gives me a place to stand and look, and a defendable reason for standing and looking.

This is why I must continue to write about animals. This is why I must write about a child who picks up a poker and kills an animal that is now almost definitely extinct.

Works Cited

Day, D. 1981. *The Doomsday Book of Animals*. London, England: Ebury Press.

Center for Biological Diversity. "Remembering the Passenger Pigeon." 2016. Accessed December 3. http://www.biologicaldiversity.org/species/birds/passenger_pigeon.

History, Council of Yukon First Nations. 2016. Accessed December 3. http://cyfn.ca/history.

Animals that Work in Stories

Lisa Johnson

W.C. Fields famously quipped, "Never work with animals or children." This may be good advice for actors. Accidents or being outdone by a too-cute colleague are perhaps the bane of performers but not of writers. Indeed, writers can do much with happy accidents and the cuteness factor. And that is just for starters. Leaving the issue of children aside, writers can employ animals in their stories strategically, doing double duty, to serve the craft of writing itself. At the same time, animals in stories can raise awareness about real issues related to animals. Of course, it goes without saying that an animal can just be an animal in a story—sometimes a cat is just a cat—but in the hands of a thoughtful and careful writer, the appearance of an animal in a story can be leveraged to convey more than the flat meaning that an animal is present.

This is not to suggest that an animal is an "ingredient" in the craft of storytelling. Indeed, the use of animals in storytelling can also elevate animals from their often-overlooked status as "other" to that reality closer to the truth—as sentient beings with complex emotional, sensate, and social lives. This essay identifies some writing tactics for ways animals have been employed by writers to serve the craft of writing, and it discusses how the use of animals in stories have helped readers see animals as authentic beings worthy of consideration in their own right.

Examples are drawn from Anna Sewell's *Black Beauty*, Beatrix Potter's *Peter Rabbit*, Richard Adams's *Watership Down*, Jack London's "The White Silence," Ian McEwan's *Black Dogs*, Mark Spragg's *Where Rivers Change Direction*, Cormac McCarthy's *The Road*, and J. M. Coetzee's *Elizabeth Costello*. These are works in which animals appear in more than tangential roles, and examination of these works can help other writers think about how they might employ animals in their own works. The primary criterion for inclusion in this discussion was that an animal appears in the piece in a non-incidental role. "Non-incidental" here does not mean "lengthy appearance." Indeed, in McCarthy's piece, the mention of a dog does not exceed two pages.

The Animal Character as a Direct Conduit for an Author's Thoughts

Anna Sewell's *Black Beauty* and Beatrix Potter's *Peter Rabbit* are works in which the respective authors have used animal characters to teach their readers about something the authors wished to convey to their audiences. To do this, they humanize the animals that appear in their stories, so the animals can convey the author's thoughts directly to the reading audience. The word "humanize" is used rather than "anthropomorphize" because modernly, the word "anthropomorphize" carries negative connotations, and no such connotations are intended here. Additionally, while Sewell's work raised awareness about the plight of working horses, the effects of Potter's work on rabbits is not so clear.

Humanization of the animals has the effect of drawing readers closer to the characters than they might otherwise be because differences between animals and humans are minimized, or fictionalized into sameness, or at least similarity. The reasoning goes something like this: If we accept the premises that animals and humans are part of nature, and that animals are seen as part of nature more readily than humans are, then we see that humanizing animals in stories has the effect of creating a linkage with nature that eliminates (or, at least, greatly diminishes) human beings' perceived separateness from nature. By not treating animals as "other" but rather as "same as us," the barrier between the animal world and the human world disappears, which renders lessons imparted from the animal characters immediately relevant to human lives.

Sewell's Black Beauty is a direct mouthpiece for the author, who was greatly concerned about the welfare of working horses. Black Beauty's role in the story is central and inseparable from the point of Sewell's writing. Sewell, through Black Beauty, directly urges compassion and sensitivity about horse welfare and misuse. As Black Beauty tells his readers:

> What I suffered with that rein ... would be hard to describe; but I am quite sure that, had it lasted much longer, either my health or my temper would have given way ... The action of the sharp bit on my tongue and jaw, and the constrained position of my head and throat, always caused

me to froth at the mouth ... [I]t is a sure sign of some discomfort, and should be attended to. Besides this, there was a pressure on my windpipe, which often made my breathing very uncomfortable. When I returned from my work, my neck and chest were strained and painful, my mouth and tongue tender, and I felt worn and depressed.

The point of Sewell's work is transparent. Humans identify with Beauty's emotions, his life struggles, and the notions of unfairness and cruelty because Beauty speaks in our language and comments on things that we can relate to. And, importantly, readers see the effects of this subjectively because they are able to identify with the horse, rather than as distant objective observers. Beauty is a spokesman from the inside. He is a horse with a voice and the power of human language. This has the effect of connecting the audience to the animal. If we recognize that an animal is "of nature," then this type of use of an animal in a story can create connections between humans and nature. More specifically to Sewell's concerns, during the time she was writing, anti-cruelty statutes were beginning to appear in the several of the United States and in England. One of the primary beneficiaries of early anti-cruelty statutes were working horses. Sewell's Beauty helped readers—including those who worked with horses—see the horse as an intelligent being, capable of feeling pain and experiencing sadness.

Potter's work also reflects the use of animals as a conduit for the author's ideas by humanizing the animal characters. As with Sewell's work, Potter's strategy creates a connection between readers and animals. This strategy creates a sense of allegiance with the characters and defeats any sense of separateness. However, while Potter uses her characters to convey her ideas, unlike Sewell's Beauty, Peter Rabbit is not a direct mouthpiece of Potter. Rather, he is a rabbit living his highly humanized life, complete with jacket, shoes, and a mother who shops for bread and makes dinner. Additionally, though Mrs. Rabbit admonishes her children not to "get into mischief," Peter "was very naughty," unlike his sisters, "who were good little bunnies." This story has many animal characters, such as the "naughty" bunny (Peter), the "good little bunnies" (the sisters, Flopsy, Mopsy, and Cotton-tail), and the wholesome mother (Mrs. Rabbit). We learn from Mrs. Rabbit that Mr. Rabbit was "put in a pie" after being caught in Mr. McGregor's garden. We are therefore left to speculate about why Peter entered the garden where his father met his demise. Perhaps Peter did not fully appreciate the danger to little rabbits who eat from the McGregor garden. Of course, this is a lesson Peter learned, after Mr. McGregor chased poor little Peter, which caused Peter fear and disorientation when he couldn't find the gate to escape. More important, the lesson imparted to the readers is that great danger exists for little ones who do not obey parental authority.

Though Peter Rabbit does not channel Potter in the same way that Beauty channels Sewell's voice, Potter's sensibilities come through clearly. This is a cautionary tale about the dangers that lie in wait for children who misbehave. Children who do not heed their mothers' warnings to stay out of mischief may, at the end of the day, find themselves feeling unwell, in bed, and missing supper, just like Peter.

Sewell's and Potter's works provide two clear strategies of how animal characters can be used by an author. First, as demonstrated by Sewell, an animal can be placed in a story as a stand-in for an author who has a message that she would like to convey about the plight of an animal. This is how Sewell very successfully helped people learn about the everyday circumstances of work horses in the nineteenth century. This strategy creates a sort of self-authenticating credibility when an animal character relays a message an animal in that position might like to relay, if only "real" animals could speak a human language.

The second strategy, demonstrated by Potter, allows an author to use animal characters to teach a lesson. Potter accomplished this by making the animal characters like people, so that readers could relate to the characters and apply those lessons to their own lives. Of course, Potter could have used human characters. Peter Rabbit could have been Peter the Boy. But animal characters have nearly universal appeal, and this is certainly true for Potter's target audience of children. Readers can trust animal characters because animals are honest. If animals learn a lesson, then it must be a lesson worth learning.

Though Potter may not have elevated the plight of rabbits in the same way that Sewell's efforts helped spread the word about working horses, it certainly may have been a catalyst for generations of children who grew up with affection for rabbits. Of course, this also has quite a downside that every writer must understand. Children's works that create a desire for certain types of animals often perpetuate the crisis of homeless pets. After all, baby bunnies (or chicks or ducklings or dalmatian puppies) grow up. Moreover, "real" animals are obviously different than animated animals. These obvious facts are somehow overlooked by some households that procure animals in response to something its members read or saw, and often this ends tragically for the innocent animal involved. When creating animal characters, writers bear a responsibility for how these characters influence readers.

The Animal Character Demonstrates Elements of the Human Condition

Richard Adams's *Watership Down* features a well-developed cast of rabbits. This is foremost a story about a journey—both literally and figuratively. Literally, the rabbits must journey to find a new place for their warren. The figurative journey travels through terrains familiar to us all: interpersonal relationships, the struggles of life, aging and youth, and goodness and evil. The rabbits are rabbits, yes, but they also belong to a rich culture that is very human-like. They face seemingly overwhelming odds to find a safe homeland, and their journey forces them to confront many facets of life that any human being would recognize. They maintain their culture through relationships, storytelling, and game-playing. For example, we learn that a traditional rabbit game includes bob-stones, which is a form of wagering involving stones. Since human readers understand gambling, and the rabbits in Adams's story use stones when gambling, a bridge is created between the human reader and the animal character. From a writer's perspective, placement of animal characters in situations that human beings recognize from their own lives is an easy way to create allegiance between the readers and the animals.

Adams seems interested in using these rabbits as proxies for exploring elements of the human condition. They grow and change much like any human character in a good story. They plan for the future, portray fear in frightful situations, and exhibit great hope, a sense of adventure, and a need for security. These are—at the *very* least—human traits. For example, during the telling of a frightful tale of the awesome

Black Rabbit who "spoke with the voice of water that falls into pools in echoing places in the dark," we hear a first-person account of the effects of the story on the rabbit listeners:

> "Hazel," said Pipkin, staring into the dusk and trembling, "I don't like this story. I know I'm not brave … "
>
> "It's all right, Hlao-roo," said Fiver, "you're not the only one." In fact he himself seemed composed and even detached, which was more than could be said for any other rabbit in the audience.

Who would not be taken back instantly to memories of their own storytelling huddles in the dark of night? Certainly this exchange reminds readers of long-ago, frightful stories around campfires, the pressing need to maintain composure for the benefit of others, and the overpowering need to make the source of fear stop. In short, readers can relate to Adams's rabbits along their journey.

Of course, this state of relation can jolt readers as Adams's deft storytelling makes them face the proverbial mirror. Some of the rabbits are fearsome indeed, which can impel a reader to examine himself to see if any such dark characteristics exist within. For example, the main-character rabbits encounter a foreign warren, whose members knowingly allow some of their numbers to be killed for food by the human landowner, in exchange for long-term security from other predators. After reading such a thing, an attentive reader could reasonably ask himself what he has traded in the name of his own security, and if the price of that trade is too high. Humans can relate to the notion of exchanging long-term safety for short-term security. It is the cost of that trade that can cause discomfort.

Writing about the human condition can be difficult, but the subject is frequently taken up by philosophers, theologians, and social scientists. Of course, not everyone reads in those disciplines, so there is great value when writers for wider audiences can do this well. One way to do this is by using animal characters as proxies for human beings. Readers tend to lean in to a story when animals are the main characters because, at the very least, animals are appealing. Writers can connect the reader and the animal character, allowing the reader to forget—at least momentarily—any sense of "otherness." In such a state, the animal condition is easily relatable to the human condition (and vice versa). Adams, of course, does this by humanizing his rabbits.

Despite Adams's undisputed contributions to the craft of writing itself and to raising awareness about rabbits, rabbits—like many other animals—are still considered personal property. In some areas, they are considered invasive species or "vermin." While his readers might have developed a fondness for rabbits, these animals also continue to be exploited in the pet industry and the food industry.

Jack London's "The White Silence" stands as a good example for a specific struggle implicit to the human condition. Namely, the story illustrates the futility of human effort to dominate nature. Victories, if they are achieved at all, are short-lived. Though London's ostensible main characters are human beings, the landscape itself is also a main character—the Great White North. But London's placement of the sled dogs, who are traveling with the humans, allow him to spin this parable on a personal scale, perhaps in a way that is more accessible than conveyance of the bare struggle of humans against the vast arctic itself.

The reader finds the sled dogs in a state of misery—starving, cold, overworked, and beaten. The human characters are ceaseless taskmasters, driving the dogs, demanding obeisance, offering no succor in exchange. The humans want what they need, and they will extract it by command or by force.

But the dogs are in dire straits. Carmen is a sled dog, and she and the other dogs feature prominently as stand-ins for nature, which is the exact "thing" the human characters are fighting against. Carmen is ultimately overcome, but the human characters do not drop the death blow. Nor can they keep her alive. Nature itself is clearly the master.

As readers, we may want to say, "Hurry up! Just get through this. Get *through* it—regardless of whether the human characters live or die." We are uncomfortable in the Great White North, and London creates this discomfort through his characters' maltreatment of the sled dogs. In the following scene, Mason lies dying while Malemute Kid waits for him to die. Human and canine characters are starving, and the temperature is freezing. Finally, the dogs (nature) threaten to overcome the humans.

> The dogs had broken the iron rule of their masters and were rushing the grub. [Malemute Kid] joined the issue with his rifle reversed ... Rifle ... went up and down, hit or missed with monotonous regularity; lithe bodies flashed, with wild eyes and ripping fangs; and man and beast fought for supremacy to the bitterest conclusion. Then the beaten brutes crept to the edge of the firelight, licking their wounds, voicing their misery to the stars.

The whole stock of dried salmon had been devoured, and perhaps five pounds of flour remained to tide them over two hundred miles of wilderness …

Morning brought fresh trouble. The animals were turning on each other. Carmen, who still clung to her slender thread of life, was downed by the pack. The lash fell among them unheeded. They cringed and cried under the blows, but refused to scatter till the last wretched bit had disappeared—bones, hide, hair, everything.

Then he beat the dogs into submission …

Nature gives up its dominance grudgingly and, we know, temporarily. Only elements of nature can be subdued—here, the sled dogs—and, again we know, temporarily. The fantasy of harboring beliefs to the contrary is fantasy:

It is not pleasant to be alone with painful thoughts in the White Silence … the bright White Silence, clear and cold, under steely skies, is pitiless.

… At high noon, the sun, without raising its rim above the southern horizon, threw a suggestion of fire athwart the heavens, then quickly drew it back … The White Silence seemed to sneer, and a great fear came upon [the Malemute Kid].

While the sled dogs might make a ready stand-in for nature so that the human characters can take their actions on them, such use of animals in stories also may risk anesthetizing readers to the violence against animals. This leads us to one of the great questions writers face when writing about animals: Do we portray human-animal relationships as they are or as we wish them to be? Clearly, London was committed to portraying the world as it was in his eyes. In the world we live in today, some animals have a degree of legal protection that did not exist during London's life. And it's reasonable to assume that these protections will expand in the years ahead, something writers need to keep in mind when they consider their audiences today and tomorrow.

The Animal Character Marks Character Growth

Some authors use animal characters—specifically *harm* those animal characters—to mark a momentous turn within the story, such as growth in a human character.

London's sled dogs are used to signify character growth. Carmen, in particular, illustrates that nature shapes us. Even if we mistreat it (or, in this case "her") terribly, we will take lessons from those interactions. For London, Carmen—like nature itself—is something to be dominated, used, and learned from. Mason, one of the human characters, commits violence against Carmen, and this episode ultimately culminates in significant character growth in Mason:

> "Don't, Mason," entreated Malemute Kid; "the poor devil's on its last legs. Wait and we'll put my team on."
>
> Mason deliberately withheld the whip till the last word had fallen, then out flashed the long lash, completely curling about the offending creature's body. Carmen—for it was Carmen—cowered in the snow, cried piteously, then rolled over on her side.

It was a tragic moment, a pitiful incident of the trail—a dying dog, two comrades in anger … Malemute Kid restrained himself, though there was a world of reproach in his eyes, and behind over the dog, cut the traces. No word was spoken.

[Mason is soon crushed by a falling tree, and Malemute Kid tends him while he is dying.]

"And Kid!" [Malemute Kid] stooped lower to catch the last faint words, the dying man's surrender of his pride. "I'm sorry—for—you know—Carmen."

Carmen represents the embodiment of the natural world, and Mason's whipping of her captures his frustration with nature itself. The whipping of Carmen is a metaphor for the struggle between man and nature. This incident makes clear the tension in the relationship between the two men, which ultimately reflects their tension with the extreme landscape through which they are traveling. The whipping of Carmen prompts a growth of character in the dying Mason, albeit on his death bed, where he surrenders his pride.

As writers, we might question the abuse of an animal in a story, just as we would question the abuse of animals in real life. Indeed, to write about animal abuse could be construed an act of violence in and of itself. The large question is one of intent. What does the writer intend for the reader to think and feel? And how does violence against animals serve this goal? Is it to raise awareness, inspire change? Or is the violence simply used for "entertainment" value?

Mark Spragg's memoir, *Where Rivers Change Direction*, is filled with animals. Here, the discussion focuses on horses.

Horses in the Spragg story are ridden, loved, roped, killed, found, and used. Indeed, he tells us in the opening paragraph, "When I was a boy my father had horses, over a hundred of them ... He believed that horses were to use." We are also told that Spragg spent much time with horses. "I haltered them ... I pinched their flanks ... I lifted their tails ... I swatted their rumps, and withers, and backs with an empty gunnysack ... I bridled them. Led them. Saddled them." Spragg used to "worry over [his] love for [horses]."

Spragg does not humanize animals. Unlike Sewell, he does not invite readers to understand the emotional lives of horses from the horses' perspectives. However, he does invite us to understand the bond between human and animal from the human perspective, and this invitation is a strength of this story. When an animal is employed to mark character growth or a significant turn in a story, the animal has to "matter" to a reader. If, as in Spragg's work, there is no other technique employed to create a connection between an animal character and a human reader, a reader must still be made to care. Writers cannot assume that readers will "automatically" care about the animal character. So, Spragg allows us to see that *he* cared, and allows us to ride that current with him, even without humanizing the animal or without trying to understand the animal from the animal's perspective.

With this understanding comes great pain, when we learn that the narrator is asked to bear-bait one of his beloved horses, Socks. This incident marks the turning point for the narrator. In short, Spragg was asked by someone that he trusted to kill the horse and to leave his body for bears, so trophy hunters could kill the bears that would be drawn to the downed horse. "I'm fifteen. Old enough to be asked," we are told. Socks is in a pitiable spot, as is the boy who is put in the position to kill him. We as readers know what it is to love at fifteen, and what it is to need to prove one's self at that age, too. We know what is going to happen before it does, and the story drags us there with the strength of an undertow.

Here Spragg uses the murder of a horse as a literary device—the killing of Socks changes his life's direction. (The common-law definition for *murder* is homicide plus malice. *Homicide* is the intentional killing of a human being. Therefore, the term *murder* might cause some readers concern because a horse is not a human being. However, stretching the definition in common parlance, such as in this writing, seems appropriate. Indeed, it seems appropriate to do so in law, though the law does not yet recognize application of the term *murder* to the taking of an animal's life because animals are considered personal property in law.) The extreme act of violence against an innocent and loved animal signifies a great change in the flow of the narrator's life. For a time, indeed, he turns his back on the ways of aspects of his upbringing. The title of the book reflects this change.

Now, we might also recognize that Socks was used to impart clarity on an element of the human condition—specifically, human beings are naturally drawn to animals and form relationships with them. Observations that one might take from Spragg's work about these relationships are many. For example, Spragg wished to convey that a necessary part of being human is to close one's heart to an animal because if one does not pull back emotional involvement, ordinary living may become unbearable. Of course, many people do pull their emotions back at a rather early age, which has led to willful ignorance and perpetuation of harm in the face of untold suffering in the food and research industries. Spragg may be suggesting that maintaining unchecked emotional connections with animals may be eventually too painful to bear, which may in turn suggest the necessity to keep the boundary line between "us" and "animal" quite impenetrable and taut.

Like Spragg's work, Ian McEwan's *Black Dogs* also uses animals to signify profound changes in his main characters' lives. Additionally, and to a much greater degree than Spragg's work, animals are blatantly "other," with no attempt by McEwan to eliminate the barrier between human and animal.

The title itself refers both to two black dogs in the story and as metaphor for random evil. The black dogs encountered by a primary character in the story ultimately serve as the catalyst that dramatically changes the course of the main character's life. Specifically, after an encounter with two hungry, menacing, large, ownerless, ex-Nazi SS dogs that were allegedly accomplices to the rape of a woman, the main character, June, utterly transforms. She turns away from the forward-looking intellectual movement of communism that she had previously shared with her husband and like-minded contemporaries, and she creates a life devoted to solitude, metaphysical study, meditation, and spiritual pursuits. As June explains it,

> that morning I came face to face with evil. I ... sensed it in my fear—these animals were the creations of debased imaginations, of perverted spirits no amount of social theory could account for. The evil I'm talking about lives in us all. It takes hold in an individual, in private lives, within a family, and then its children ... And then, when the conditions are right, in different countries, at different times, a terrible cruelty, a

viciousness against life erupts, and everyone is surprised by the depth of hatred within himself. Then it sinks back and waits. It's something in our hearts.

McEwan's black dogs are a pivotal point for this character. June quite literally changes her life's course after encountering these dogs. For example, she directly addresses the fact that "social theory" cannot account for pure evil. Instead of pursuing the changes promised by the communist movement that had so inspired her before, she realized that such hope is for naught. Evil "sinks back and waits" for "when the conditions are right," regardless of the good work that social theory might do in the interim.

Bernard, June's husband, acknowledges June's interpretation of the black dogs, though he disagrees with it mightily. Building upon Churchill's description of his own depression as his "black dog", Bernard notes that June's idea was that if one dog was a personal depression, two dogs were a kind of cultural depression, "civilization's worst moods." Rejecting this interpretation, Bernard chooses to regard the situation in non-metaphysical terms. Simply, two dogs frightened June. Nevertheless, it is June's musings that capture McEwan's readers:

> There was a certain irreducible respect owed by dogs to humans, bred over generations, founded upon the unquestionable facts of human intelligence and dog stupidity. And on dogs' celebrated loyalty, their dependency, their abject desire to be mastered. But out here the rules were exposed as mere convention, a flimsy social

contract. Here, no institutions asserted human ascendancy. There was only the path, which belonged to any creature that could walk it.

In this way, McEwan is able to transform the fact of these dogs into a turning point for his characters who encountered them. June's life's focus shifted dramatically. For Bernard, he became more entrenched in his commitment to practical or grounded explanations and things that could be fixed with due diligence. Significantly, Bernard did not actually see the black dogs, but instead, he

> [f]ound [June] a quarter of an hour later sitting on the path ... [S]he said tersely that she had been frightened by two dogs and she wanted to turn back. He did not see the bloodied knife, and June forgot to pick it up.

This last excerpt does double duty. June wanted to turn back that day from the actual trail upon which they were walking, but she also wanted to turn back from the path that had so occupied the trajectory of her life. And she did. Bernard did not see the actual bloodied knife that June had used to defend herself, but he also did not see the symbolism of the bloody knife: the demise of their life plans together.

Like Spragg, McEwan does not invite the reader to connect with the black dogs. Those dogs—at least according to June—represented pure evil. Metaphorically, McEwan is discussing social evils. This may not be something that people can truly "connect" with. But observe? Yes.

Interestingly, McEwan's character Bernard also uses animals in the same way that McEwan uses them. That is, they are devices that signify change. For instance, Bernard finds a beautiful red dragonfly, and he wishes to preserve it for study. June refuses to be complicit in the death of the creature at first, but then she relinquishes. She is observed by Bernard as going "cold and logical" when she discovers that he wants to kill it, and she said, "It's beautiful, therefore you want to kill it." This interaction with the dragonfly is used to signify change in Bernard. He explains, "All I was interested in was abstraction. I claimed to love 'creation,' as she called it, but in fact I wanted to control it, choke the life out of it, label it, arrange it in rows." The author has used the intentional destruction of an animal as a turning point for a main character. Bernard is able to reflect deeply upon the deficiencies in equating love with control. Additionally, we see Bernard originally conceiving of an animal as something to dominate. This hearkens back to the earlier discussion of the use of animals by a writer to demonstrate aspects of the human condition.

Since we cannot know how everyone reads the same story, writerly awareness about the tradeoffs between the use of animals to convey ideas and the points that can be taken from that use must be considered. For example, a misreading of McEwan might suggest that black dogs are inherently evil. Of course, that is not correct, but people have sometimes formed unfortunate opinions about animals based upon their characterization in literature and cultural superstitions. And people are less likely to adopt black cats and dogs because of these superstitions. Consider, for example, the evil imputed to snakes or "serpents" and the serpent's role in the story of Adam and Eve.

The Animal Character Signifies a Loss of Nature, or the Loss of Human Attachment to Nature

The loss of human attachment to nature or the loss of nature itself can suggest a loss of humanity. A loss of humanity can make way for or even beckon evil. Cormac McCarthy's *The Road* follows a man and his young son in a post-(probably) nuclear-event world as they travel toward a vague and unknowable destination. This work throbs with the loss of nature in a bleak, desolate, and frightening landscape where human manifestation of evil is not uncommon.

McCarthy's animals are dogs, but his dogs do not appear in the flesh in this story. Instead, they are presented distantly in each instance they are mentioned. For example, one dog is presented as a far-off sound, and the man and his young son discuss it:

> What was that?
> I didn't hear anything.
> Listen.
> I don't hear anything.
> They listened. Then in the distance he heard a dog bark. He turned and looked toward the darkening town. It's a dog, he said.
> A dog?
> Yes.
> Where did it come from?
> I don't know.
> We're not going to kill it, are we Papa?
> No. We're not going to kill it.
> He looked down at the boy. Shivering in his coats. He bent over and kissed him on his gritty brow. We won't hurt the dog. I promise.

[The man and the boy sleep.]
They never heard the dog again.

This is a real-time experience for these characters. The first concern from the child is whether the dog will be killed. As we know from other parts of this story, this child has never experienced pre-apocalyptic nature or animals of any kind, except for other humans. Though the son expresses concern about the dog itself, we might also see that the child is asking a representative of the generation that killed nature whether he intends to do the same thing to one of the last remaining vestiges of it, which has made "itself" known in the form of a dog.

Later, another dog is presented as a memory, as the man recounts an event that occurred before the reader enters the story:

> The dog that [the boy] remembers followed us for two days. I tried to coax it to come but it would not. I made a noose of wire to catch it. There were three cartridges in the pistol. None to spare. She walked away down the road. The boy looked after her and then he looked at me and then he looked at the dog and he began to cry and to beg for the dog's life and I promised I would not hurt the dog. A trellis of a dog with the hide stretched over it. The next day it was gone. That is the dog he remembers. He doesn't remember any little boys.

There, McCarthy's character's first instinct may have been

to kill the dog (nature) with a noose—likely given their extremely precarious food shortage—but the child uncovers the plot quickly and extracts a promise from his father not to do it. This is an interesting exchange because we know that these two human characters are starving, and, therefore, some might argue they have a compelling reason to kill the dog. Yet it also begs the question as to whether the other "compelling" human reasons that existed as humans killed nature *en masse* were also avoidable, if they could have seen the faces of the next generation crying and begging them not to hurt it.

In other instance, a likeness of a dog is offered as a sad rendition of what has been lost. We learn that "everything [was] covered in ash. A child's room with a stuffed dog on the windowsill looking out at the garden." A sense of loss is invoked by the dog and the garden—both archetypal symbols—one of fidelity and the other of bounty. In *The Road*, everything green is gone, and we are left to imagine the darkness and utter waste that the stuffed dog "sees" now, as the human characters encounter it, sitting on its sill.

Without nature, humans cannot live, as the excerpt below illustrates. As the boy's parents argue the virtues of suicide or life, we learn that the boy's mother favors death. McCarthy creates a perverse hope in his reader for the end of existence to come for those characters, and to come quickly. They have lost or are at the precipice of losing their humanity:

> We're survivors, he told her ...
> Survivors? she said.
> Yes.
> ... We're not survivors. We're the walking dead
> ...
> I am begging you. I'll do anything.

Such as what? I should have done it a long time ago ... And now I am done ... It's the right thing to do ... We used to talk about death, she said. We don't do that anymore. Why is that?
I don't know.
It's because it's here. There's nothing left to talk about ...

The hundred nights they'd sat up debating the pros and cons of self-destruction with the earnestness of philosophers chained to a madhouse wall. In the morning the boy said ... She's gone isn't she? And he said: Yes, she is.

Coetzee also focuses on death and the loss of humanity in *Elizabeth Costello*. He uses animals that are killed by humans as his vehicle to convey his message that humans' utter disconnection with animals not only represents a loss of humanity but also affirmatively represents evil. Specifically, humans who purposefully create life so that those animals will suffer, be fearful, and ultimately be killed are humans who are practicing pure evil. Coetzee's voice is direct, like that of Sewell's. However, Coetzee does not create humanized animals to carry his message. He uses a person—his title character— as a conduit for this message. Humanity's disconnection from the suffering of animals ushers in not only the idea of a loss of human goodness but the actual presence of evil. Here we see the title character conversing at the university president's dinner table:

"But your own vegetarianism, Mrs. Costello," says President Garrard, pouring oil on troubled

> waters: "it comes out of a moral conviction, does
> it not?"
>
> "No, I don't think so," says [Elizabeth Costello].
> "It comes out of a desire to save my soul."

Elizabeth Costello equates her non-participation in the consumption of meat with religious overtones. She asks, "A sparrow knocked off a branch by a slingshot, a city annihilated from air: who dare say which is the worse? Evil, all of it, an evil universe invented by an evil god."

Coetzee's words virtually always do double duty, and these instances are no exception. Here, for instance, we can see how he sets up sparrows (the light, literally "winged" goodness) against Satan (here called "the evil god"). Many mystics who seek God within abstain from eating meat due to their commitment to peace and their resistance to adding karmic debt to hinder their way toward God. Moreover, many mystics see the Earth itself as a creation of Satan, who creates this reality that is wholly separate from the light of God (with a capital "G"). In this way, we can see that Costello's reference to "an evil god" (with a lowercase "g") quite probably refers to Satan. In this short span, Coetzee signals the presence of actual evil—in the flesh—by using an animal (the sparrow) as a device to usher it in to his story.

Coetzee's Costello also equates the genocide committed against animals on a daily basis as a modern-day version of the horrors of the Holocaust.

> Let me say it openly: we are surrounded by an
> enterprise of degradation, cruelty, and killing
> which rivals anything that the Third Reich
> was capable of, indeed dwarfs it, in that ours

is an enterprise without end, self-regenerating, bringing rabbits, rats, poultry, livestock ceaselessly into the world for the purpose of killing them.

Here is another excerpt—perhaps the most memorable in this story—concerning the presence of evil as seen by the disconnection of humanity from the suffering of animals. Costello's son has just asked her why she has "become so intense about the animal business."

> I seem to move around perfectly easily among people, to have perfectly normal relations with them. Is it possible, I ask myself, that all of them are participants in a crime of stupefying proportions? Am I fantasizing it all? I must be mad! Yet every day I see the evidence. The very people I suspect produce the evidence, exhibit it, offer it to me. Corpses. Fragments of corpses that they have bought for money.
>
> It is as if I were to visit friends, and to make some polite remark about the lamp in their living room, and they were to say, "Yes, it's nice isn't it? Polish Jewish skin it's made of, we find that's best, the skins of young Polish-Jewish virgins." And then I go to the bathroom and the soap wrapper says, "Treblinka — 100% human stearate."

Costello expounds on the connection between people and animals, which undergirds her belief that this connection not be lost:

... we are all of one kind [humans and animals], one nature ... children all over the world consort quite naturally with animals. They don't see any dividing line. That is something they have to be taught, just as they have to be taught it is all right to kill and eat them.

Both Coetzee and McCarthy employ animals to give us a glimpse of not only what has been lost but what we have exchanged for the connection that we might have once had with animals (pure evil).

If a writer wishes to write about nature, animals, particularly those classified as "wildlife," can be ready symbols for it. McCarthy chose an animal—a dog—that is not "wildlife" but probably feral, and it worked, because the dog links the loss of nature and the loss of domesticated humanity at a glimpse. Likewise, Coetzee chose "farm animals" rather than wildlife, but it works because he is able to link willful indifference to suffering—human or animal—as a manifestation of evil, and such a presence diminishes humanity and separates us from our very nature and from nature itself.

The Animal Character Foreshadows Plot

Carmen is cruelly felled by a whip that she is powerless to stop; Mason is crushed by a falling tree that he cannot escape. These events illustrate the unchanging nature of one of London's main characters—the landscape. The Malemute Kid's appeal to forego the whipping of Carmen reflects the realization that London's human (and possibly canine) characters eventually reach. Namely, raging against nature's forces achieves nothing other than expenditure of energy that cannot be easily restored, particularly with exhausted food stores. Similarly, whether or not Malemute Kid had bent to hear Mason's apology, nature itself would have devoured it. Indeed, it seems that nature swiftly paid Mason in-kind for his maltreatment of Carmen by crushing and then devouring him. Perhaps London recognized the futility of individualism (like whipping a dog to "make" the dog do something) because interactions with nature are inherently deterministic.

Ian McEwan employs rabbits in *Black Dogs*—the violence against which foreshadows plot. For instance, he uses a "heap of bloodied fur," which turns out to be a rabbit, as a foreshadowing device for an episode of parental violence against a small boy, and an episode in which the narrator, Jeremy, steps forward to avenge it, as well as the long-ago violence against his much younger sister. A "heap of bloodied fur" is obviously the sign of an act of violence upon an animal, and this symbol of violence signifies change in Jeremy, who is finally able to avenge his sister's maltreatment. Interestingly, when Jeremy is called off from beating the other party, the same words are used on him that are used to calm dogs in the story: "*Ca suffit.*" Likewise, June and Bernard are rabbits. June describes her and Bernard's youth: "And I was with the man I loved and we were rabbiting on about how we were going to help change the world." Rabbits are once again used in foreshadowing. Specifically, when Jeremy and Bernard are at the Berlin Wall when it falls, they see "dozens of rabbits, searching out fringes of grass to nibble" in the area where land mines were buried, and one of the men comments to the other, "Their time is almost up." The mines are signals of imminent violence against the animals, which signifies extreme change in politics, and politics is a character in this book. Likewise, it seems that June and Bernard were out of their warrens, so to speak, naïve like rabbits, and unbeknownst to them, waiting to be pounced on by the evil lurking in the world, embodied by McEwan's black dogs.

McEwan also uses a scorpion to foreshadow a philosophical debate between the disembodied voices in Jeremy's head. These voices belong to June and Bernard, arguing for faith and skepticism, respectively. Unlike the other animals in this story, we are not told the outcome of the change in Jeremy, or even if there was one, as a result of the encounter with the scorpion. Jeremy has inexplicable fear as he tries to find the light fuse box in the dark. As it turns out, the scorpion was located exactly where he would have placed his hand if he had listened to the "rational" voice in his head rather than the "spiritual warning" that he seemed to also be receiving. Readers might be able to surmise that this foreshadowed Jeremy's willingness to listen to the spiritual rather than simply the logical, though the readers are not given any further glimpses.

A primary danger of employing animals to foreshadow events is slotting an animal into a human-projected characteristic. This can do no favors for the animals in question, and it may run the risk of cliché. For example, a writer who wishes to foreshadow a sly move by a main character may want to think very carefully before inserting a fox in a fore-scene.

When Writing with Animals

Every nonhuman animal you employ in your writing deserves just as much consideration as the human characters. Before writing an animal into your work, consider some basic questions.

What is your purpose for including the animal?

- Is the animal simply there because animals exist in our world? This most casual of inclusions might yet serve another purpose. For example, imagine a writer who employs an owl's *whoo-whoo*. This writer might only wish to reflect the owl's presence. But the owl's presence helps to sketch the visual or auditory landscape of that specific scene.

- Does the animal serve a structural element of the story? When developing important components of the story, such as character, setting, plot, conflict, or theme, consider whether an animal can carry some of this work. For example, as readers, we do not need for London to tell us that the human struggle against nature will ultimately fail, despite some ability to dominate it in the short run. Instead, we might reach that conclusion on our own after reflecting on Carmen and the other starving sled dogs. Such planning can also help a writer sidestep tendencies to write too "on the nose." For example, readers do not need Spragg to tell us that ranch life can be exploitative of innocents. Instead, we might reach that conclusion ourselves, after reading about Spragg's boyhood and bear-baiting.

- Clarify whether an animal character might serve as your mouthpiece. If so, decide the substance of the message that you wish to share with your readers. Like any character, an animal character can speak plainly about your intended message, like Sewell's Black Beauty, or can convey messages indirectly, like Potter's Peter Rabbit.

- Consider what the animal symbolizes. If there is some

well-known trait associated with the animal that you wish to write, consider whether that animal can be a stand-in or a deepener for some aspect of theme, or can be used to foreshadow. For example, McCarthy leveraged widely accepted ideas about dogs to convey loss, a primary theme in *The Road*. Specifically, the ideas of loyalty and "man's best friend" were conveyed both by the toy dog "gazing" at the lost garden, and the actual dogs in the distance, unreachable, unknowable, and—most important—un-huntable.

- Consider whether the presence of the animal character helps or hinders the writing. For example, if the human character has a companion dog, the dog's presence is likely unremarkable. But if the human character keeps a pet Humboldt penguin, the reader will likely be distracted with questions unintended by the author. If the writing concerns the penguin pet trade, or if the penguin serves some structural component of the story, then such a choice makes sense. But if not, such a choice will set readers up for frustration.

Is the animal portrayed authentically?

- Is the animal portrayed as other members of the species? If the animal character is presented without extraordinary characteristics that are not observed in "real-life" animals, then the animal's presence in a story can educate readers about the species in general, or about individual members of a certain species in particular. Additionally, human-animal relationships might be portrayed as they are, even when those interactions are unpleasant. This allows a writer to convey brutal facts without writing gratuitous violence. For example, in "real life," chickens are not required by law to be stunned before slaughter. Consequently, factory-farmed chickens suffer tortuous deaths. Writing the rough truth about the actual slaughter of chickens in factory farming differs starkly from writing simply for the purpose of writing violence.

- Is the animal is portrayed authentically? If an animal is speaking a human language, wearing clothing, driving cars, or doing anything at all that differs from "real-life" animals, then the animal is not portrayed authentically. Consider the purpose that such an animal might serve in your story. For example, a writer might wish animal characters to convey some message about the human condition in a palatable manner, or to convey some message about human-animal relationships worthy of reconsideration. Adams does both deftly in *Watership Down*.

Consider the many possibilities for asking animal characters to work in your stories. As mere presences or as central roles, they can carry subtext, themes, symbolism, creative theses, or a variety of other "story cargo." As a writer, ignore W.C. Fields' advice. People like animals. People like good writing. Try putting the two together.

WORKS CITED

Adams, Richard. 1972. *Watership Down*. New York: MacMillan Publishing Co. Inc.

Coetzee, J. M. 2003. *Elizabeth Costello*. New York: The Penguin Group.

London, Jack. 1900. "The White Silence." *Five Great Short Stories*, unabridged edition. Edited by Stanley Appelbaum. New York: Dover Publications, Inc.

McCarthy, Cormac. 2007. *The Road*. New York: Alfred A. Knopf.

McEwan, Ian. 1992. *Black Dogs*. New York: Nan A. Talese Doubleday.

Potter, Beatrix. 1902. *The Tale of Peter Rabbit*. London: Frederick Warne & Co.

Sewell, Anna. 1945. *Black Beauty: The Autobiography of a Horse*. New York: Grosset & Dunlap.

Spragg, Mark. 1945. *Where Rivers Change Direction*. Salt Lake City: The University of Utah Press.

A Case for More Reality in Writing *for* Animals

Rosemary Lombard

Ever since our childhood experience of stories like *Goldilocks and the Three Bears*, we have tapped into the long and lively tradition of animal stories that use the animal image only to put human characters in furs—or shells or scales or some other exterior sign of "animal." But *Goldilocks* is not a bear story; it is a human story. Mr. and Mrs. Bear and child, generally portrayed in human dress, form a cohesive human-like family, living together in their rectilinear, stick-built house furnished with separate beds with their dear little coverlets.

Their storied responses to the intruder are quite unlike those of their wild exemplars. Imagine setting up a camera in a bear den. Before you're done, Ma Bear and cub return. That's a bear story you might not be able to tell. Still, these extended metaphors of a child's life are used for stimulating children's social development and/or the stimulation of their reading interests and imaginations—and, I would like to think, acceptance of others with different ways and different colors of skin. As such, even with the human-like characters in costume, this type of story has its own purpose and usefulness.

However, for those of us who are concerned about wild populations of animals, the relationships of animals and humans, and the knotty issues around human uses of animals—real animals—I suggest that our approach to writing take a different path, whether we write nonfiction or fiction, even the more fluid realms of fantasy and poetry.

Our concern and respect—and, yes, love—for all life in our complex web of interdependency comes down to this: We are the literate communicators to our own species *for* animals, that is, primarily for the benefit of the animals. With all of our writers' skill, we aim to reveal the specificity of the others: the characteristics of species and individuals as honestly as we can to persuade readers of their value and needs.

The organizations whose goal is to save species know the power of love for a single animal or their chosen subset of animals and take advantage of it, whether they're soliciting donations or enlisting the help of local communities. Stephen Jay Gould said it well: "We cannot win this battle to save species and environments without forging an emotional bond between ourselves and nature as well—for we will not fight to save what we do not love."

As an animal behaviorist/cognitive psychologist, I am perhaps too sensitive to misunderstandings about my research species, turtles, but it gives me a jolt when basic facts are ignored in a context told in a way that we are led to believe is literal. An example: Does a nesting water turtle emerge to gather grasses—no—for her nest *on* the ground—no—and does she pile—no—her leathery—no—eggs on it—no—as a poet described in a context that seems to be straight description? If so, then what would we expect? The fierce little turtle mother is supposed to bare her "teeth" at the hungry raccoon? I'd be the first to say that turtles are intelligent, but how could an animal as feet-to-earth grounded as a turtle "gather" grasses or place her initially soft eggs in a pile? Anyone who thinks about the basic exterior anatomy of a turtle or has seen a video showing a sea turtle digging her nest with her back feet and laying her eggs into the sculpted hole can spot the misunderstandings.

Bright youngsters, often eager students of anything animal, can have doubts about details in a story, even in a fanciful surround. One astute four-year-old I know pointed to the three hairs sticking out of the head of Dr. Seuss's Yertle the Turtle. "Agree that it is imaginary," he said, "but it is careless." I got a similar complaint that the Teenage Mutant Ninja Turtles didn't have tails.

It's hard to guess which species characteristics a reader will expect to be true in fictional animals that differ from the real thing in form, habitat, and behavior. So often they are hardly more than bearers of their name. So how do you make your animal character authentic or, in its fantasy form, seem authentic? Or are the members of the Teenage Mutant Ninja Turtles clan and other non-animal animals so far gone from reality that, even if we want to, we cannot identify with them as animals?

I submit that we must work to approach reality more closely. Especially in those informative asides, where readers expect it straight, we need to give it to them straight. Not only do we want to prevent eye rolling from hyperliteral readers and critics, but we want to build trust with our readers—as well as satisfying ourselves and enhancing our agendas.

I recommend starting with a realistic model. If we are to believe in our animal hero or other animal characters as animals—or representing animals, even if they then stray from reality—we need to establish true and characteristic details of, say, bearness. As Gilbert of Gilbert and Sullivan told us, details "give artistic verisimilitude to an otherwise bald and unconvincing narrative." Imagine what details supporting verisimilitude do to an otherwise rich and convincing narrative! After all, the character must, at end, be convincing enough that our readers make the transfer back to the real animals we aim to protect. To that end, we need to know the lives and behavior of those animals.

The process of learning to know the animals is similar to writing about our own species. The research is like doing historical research as a background for story, yet, in fiction, having the freedom to depart from it in some ways. Likewise, structuring animal characters is similar to structuring human characters, creating a suite of characteristics of body, place, and behavior, but realistic details are even more important because of one huge, obvious difference: The animals, except a few in communication training, don't share our language. Their repertoire consists of gestures, vocalizations, scent, postures, eye/pupil change, and more; some of that we can learn. You can also use talking animals, put words in their thoughts, or have humans talk about them, but each of those choices also involves knowing the animals well, including details of appearance, place, and behavior.

Is your character, say, a bear, living in a habitat where the real species could live? Beyond appearance, a study in itself, what do you know about bears' lives, such as the cycle of their year, the young, their behaviors (for different ages, genders, and roles), their reproduction, what they smell like, their perception, their vocalizations? Especially, what do you know about communication signals, scents, or poses, intentional or not, that can communicate to others—to their own species, other animals, or us? The more you know, the more resources you have: for story, for movements, for communication, for relationships—and the more we can connect with them.

Early in Yoko Tawada's *Memoirs of a Polar Bear*, she gives us the details she chose to characterize the mother bear: how the mother bear writes the memories of her infancy—her awkward stumbles, the taste of her mother's milk, her love of the ice-cold water her trainer hosed over her. Polar bears love cold water? Indeed. Early memories in a polar bear? We can't know. Perhaps the veracity of that kind of detail doesn't matter in its context of a bear's memoir, but what other details could be chosen that come out of the natural history and speak, exclusively, "bear"? Even so, the contrast is vivid when we suddenly see that bear, now grown, standing at the window in her hotel room.

The explanation in *Memoirs of a Polar Bear* that sounds the most scientific, how polar bears stay warm, is interesting but only partly true (understandable in the scientists' morass of varied and incorrect explanations of how that works). But recent scientific evidence is not what anyone would expect and may be too complex to explain in a novel. That's a problem for authors. For each detail we have to decide: What is true, and what is important to the purpose of the story? Does what happens later require an understanding of the whole explanation? Can we explain the whole truth without losing readers? Certainly the thickness of the coat and the description of the hairs are part of the explanation and central to "bearness." That much could be included in a children's book, but how the bear gets warm and stays that way is not from the sun, but more like this: The warmth is metabolic warmth from inside the polar bear, and the super-thick coat, with those hollow and nearly transparent hairs, insulates by scattering and absorbing radiant heat. Perhaps that—or part of it—is not too arcane, but there's a danger of getting too long or technical; it depends on your readership and pace. The example speaks to the importance of dredging out the most accurate information we can but analyzing its use with care.

The trick for Tawada's book was to find the true details that service the characterization, in her case, of wild versus human-like bears and a bear-like human, important for a book whose essence plays with the ideas of human-animal relationships, with both species becoming so close that they seem to cross or exchange their usual lines.

What a human is in relation to "the others," after all, is one of those basic questions that keeps intriguing us, critically important because attitudes about our relationship to the animals profoundly affect our behavior toward them and their protection. That we are members of the larger tribe of animals and must thus be responsible to the whole is central to our purposes in writing for animals. Our species can no longer think it is the always superior, only important one, apart from the rest of the animal world, the species that may wield its power to use and abuse other animals and the environment only for short-term human purposes.

These heartfelt truths have been repeated enough that more people are getting it. Many others need the gentle persuasion of more authentic story to build a sense of equality and identity with our co-travelers.

For authenticity, it's difficult to match nonfiction that comes out of an informed and curious author who is in the story, experiencing it. In this passage from *The Animal Dialogues* by Craig Childs, we learn with lively and memorable metaphor intriguing details about what porcupines do and the adaptations enabling that behavior; but, on the next level we become, in a sense, one with Childs as he crawls toward a particular porcupine to meet her nose to nose: "It looks like a mop, a bundle of ponderosa pine needles, a mobile hairstyle. It takes a while to find the front end, the side with the two dark eyes. Teddy bear eyes and a short snout. Doesn't give a damn, just stays there and watches me as I crawl closer ... If I could ever be this calm, I think, if I could ever lay myself down on a fallen aspen and be so quiet, then I would know something."

Children's picture books by Joanne Ryder and Lynne Cherry take identity with the animal even further. For example, in *Chipmunk Song*, their collaboration of lyric poetry and well-researched illustrations of the habitat and its animals, they invite the child to "imagine you are someone small" and picture a child scaled to the size of a chipmunk and curled up asleep on a cache of fallen acorns in a chipmunk's underground burrow—just like one nearby where a sleeping chipmunk lies.

Some approaches use devices of intelligent animal speech to break down the animal-human communication barrier. Ted Kerasote and his dog Merle, a dog with independence and character, lived in a place where a dog could roam without fences or restraints, going in or out as he pleased, but what pleased him was often to be Ted's companion. Kerasote, in his *Merle's Door: Lessons from a Freethinking Dog*, shows keen awareness of a dog's—and this particular dog's—interests, perceptions, and nonverbal communication. Based on those understandings, he narrates the dog's actions and expressions, interpreting them in words: a sort of interspecies translation.

Putting my nose to his head, I'd smell perfume, occasionally cigarette smoke, other times fried food. He'd been visiting neighbors.

"You've been two-timing me, haven't you?"

He'd laugh. "What's a dog to do if he gets left at home?"

By the way, if you know or are researching dogs, you'll recognize dog laughter not as the pulled-up-and-back mouth rather like our laughs but an open-mouthed, soft *huh-huh* with the tongue laid over the teeth.

In the more literal world of many other writers, including Kathleen Dean Moore, environmental essayist and novelist, dogs don't talk, even by translation. "I don't know what to say to a dog," she says in *Holdfast: At Home in the Natural World*.

"So, how was your day," I venture. "Roll in anything disgusting?" This conversation the dogs find fascinating. They edge closer and lift their noses, as if they think they could understand English if they could just smell it better.

I've tried writing persona poems, helping turtles to speak for themselves, which then speak for the causes of their species. It helps that the species and individuals I chose for the poems have been friends for years in our collaborative exploration of their minds. The question is, "What would Turtle say?" I think box turtle Diode would say with some indignation, "I am not an it!" and that finds its way into type.

In "Pancake Tortoise Out of Africa," from my *Turtles All the Way: Poems*, I wrote in a tortoise's voice about the way he was smuggled from East Africa, sold to a boy in a Chicago pet

62

store, and, after fighting with the boy's box turtle, was to be sold again. The tortoise who inspired the poem had come to me in 1973 through the Chicago Herpetological Society. The poem, a narrative rant by the tortoise, emerged from my anger about the trade in wild animals—such a terrible problem for individual animals and the teetering status of many species. It came, too, from having learned about methods of the illicit trade in wildlife—in particular, turtles and the way they are treated in transit—and I knew the Chicago part of the story from the boy who bought him from the pet store. The poem begins like this:

I fought with his turtle, the Boy complained,
and so I must be sold.

Fighting? Why not? Uprooted from under
my African rocks, stacked with turtles all thrust
like me into a binding, blinding box, closed

and dark as the hand that plucked me from my
life,
a hand that should feel in me the pain of his
people
sent in chains from home.

Our journey of fear was torture ...

then jolts and hums of rolling machines,
screaming at times as if caught by hyenas,
and a machine that roared, more chilling than
the lion ...

Who could return to golden grass
and rocky hills of home? ...

I've tried to include something from the tortoise's perspective about habitat; something about the Africans (expert at finding these animals in the rock crevices for the wildlife traders); the fearful sounds of local predators, which provide emotional similes for the lorries and airplane; and, further on in the passage, rather gross descriptions about the horrors of the transport. At the pet store he is perplexed by magical lights, "from day to night in a moment," and the "invisible cliffs" of the glass tanks. The people in the pet store have a role: to describe the unusual shape of the species.

I think you can see that writing for animals is not exclusively natural history description, though some of the best of it is and has the advantage that, in its bare reality, it doesn't need the reader's translation from fictional animals back to the actual animals we are concerned with. Fantasy or other kinds of fiction that bend the letter of the real can, at their best, succeed at another kind of truth and, like nonfiction, create the emotional connections with the animal characters that can change our readers for the benefit of the animals. Of course, in all types of animal writing we *use* material from what we find is real.

Passages from *Walking the High Ridge*, by lepidopterist Robert Michael Pyle, show how observation, description, and research can and sometimes should move from nonfiction to fiction, for, as he notes, "Some questions can be closed in on through experimentation and close, attentive observation. Others yield to the imagination in concert with the colors, the smells, the cold crush of the stones and the soft lift of the high alpine air itself."

Pyle had long been fascinated with the large black butterfly of Colorado's alpine zone, the "Magdalena," *Erebia magdalena*, and had devised a way to test the males' response to superhero—oversized—females by flying black models down the heights in a semi-controlled way. The adventure of his account is riveting, but he was also translating his experiences into a novel, *Magdalena Mountain*. This is from the year 2000 version quoted in *Walking the High Ridge*:

> On the morning following the storm, Erebia crept up the damp walls of his nocturnal shelter, clinging to each granite grain with his tarsi, and emerged into a sunny morning. His receptors buzzed to the warm and perfectly polarized light of a cloudless sky. Several minutes of basking on his side against the black lichens warmed his flight muscles enough to work. As long as he lay there, he was cryptic against the surface. Then, at the moment his body reached the magic temperature, he launched into flight and became anything but invisible against the indigo sky.
>
> He began half way up the rockslide ... He flew directly upslope, toward the zenith. Upon reaching the ridge, he was swept up on a morning updraft ...

A few pages later, the male encounters a female. The ingredients of detailed observation and research merged with invention and structure become warp and weft of story, and we are drawn into the life of a butterfly.

In her environmental novel *Piano Tide*, Kathleen Dean Moore underlays people and plot with the animal and plant life of the southeastern Alaska coast she knows so well, which, along with water and rain, create a rich sense of place in a village built on a boardwalk above the changing tides.

> [The humpback whales] all sucked bright day into their lungs, blew it out with the sound of a rock slide. Then there was silence except for the whispers of murrelets and the flicks of the fins of wounded fish, fluttering in small circles …

Sometimes the sounds, scents, and behaviors of even the smallest creatures add to the texture of being there; sometimes, like the whales and salmon, the animals move to the fore, notably, in Moore's device of telling the coho salmons' life history in three poetic sections introducing the three parts of the book, an overview that grounds an understanding of the species' significance throughout the story.

> Cold water flows through the dark spaces between grains of gravel where the eggs have come to rest—a hundred red beads among the gray stones, sparks of life in the dark. Over time, months and months, the red fades, and each globe takes on the shape of a tiny fish with a yolk sac on its belly. More translucent than stray light, smaller than a spruce needle, it shivers there in the interstices of the stones …

When we write nonfiction, I do not mean that we abandon the richness of fictional writing styles (though we have to pay attention, too, to the expectations of our genre and our audience). As you will see in Charles Finn's descriptions below, the precise word is all the more important, and vivid figurative language can be the key to a depth of understanding and, yes, heart: that key component of persuasive writing. With Finn, a keen observer of animals and a master of vivid description and apt metaphor, you can love and respect the bear he encounters at the same time you fear it. This selection from Finn's essay about a black bear in his *Wild Delicate Seconds: 29 Wildlife Encounters* is one of my bibles of models for fine nonfiction writing about animals.

> … and a sickle moon flies. A black bear crashes through the forest. She is snapping twigs, breaking branches, a pear-shaped hole in the night. She moves in a straight line, head down, shoulders rolling, her massive behind fat from the neighbor's apples pilfered this fall. It's like watching a stone tumble downhill and I stand on my front porch shivering, inarticulate words like startled grouse exploding from my throat.
>
> When the bear stops, she is thirty paces away, her black coat gilded silver by the moon's austere light. I watch her rise on hind legs. I imagine she gives a blackberry roar.
>
> "I've seen the nap you take in the sun." I find my voice and remind her …
>
> … [S]he answers with a wag of her head … I watch her turn and plow like a fullback into the night. I go back inside.
>
> I put my frying pan down.

Setting, lighting, action, "bearness," attempted connection, human emotions, human responses. This essay has it all, starting with intense observation molded into the direct language of strong words integrated with unusual but context-appropriate metaphors. Every time I read that ending, when he puts the frying pan down, I realize I've been holding my breath.

In building a character, most times it works well to spread out details of appearance and behavior of your animal characters within the action, layering in relevant characteristics when the story needs them. If you're hinting at what's to come, that needed prescient detail, of course, can bow in early. Normally, you'll want to avoid the information dump unless you're writing a natural history field guide, which is all about dense information.

However, some writers deliberately ignore this common advice and throw all the researched characteristics and behaviors into the first appearance of the character; but note: They are clumped in for only the first draft. In the second draft, details are parsed out with care into the action for the perfect, most relevant spot.

Sometimes there is a reason to introduce a character accompanied by a large part of his author's list of characteristics. A minor character, like the yippy Jack Russell in the next block, would have a short list. He doesn't need much more unless he plays a bigger role. A major character may burst onto the scene in a way that it does seem appropriate for him or her to meet the readers fairly well characterized, or perhaps the story revolves around a character who is out of sight for much of the book. Both circumstances are true in Mindy Mejia's novel *The Dragon Keeper*. But note well: Hers is not the kind of introduction that keeps the character standing there while the description goes on and on. In this selection, Mejia introduces Jata, a zoo animal, with mystery and a sense of action.

At first she was just a bust, some kind of sculpture made out of copper running to green. Her square snout protruded out from the shadows, and she tasted the air with a flick of forked yellow, confirming what had woken her from her nap. Chicken. It flashed from her tongue to her eyes, which darted immediately to where the mini-door opened into the restraint box. Climbing out of the cave in two giant lunges, Jata broke into the open space in dead pursuit of a free lunch.

This was the best part, watching Jata walk. Did those European explorers feel the same awe when they caught their first glimpse of a Komodo dragon? Jata walked diagonally, one foot in time with the opposite hind leg, in a sweeping, swaggering motion. Her tail pumped out behind her like a three-foot-long, bone-encrusted rudder, stirring up dirt and leaves and even a few wadded-up napkins in her wake. Sweep, swagger, she walked. Sweep, swagger, and even though her head bobbed up and down in time, her eyes never moved; they had locked in on the restraint-box door. She passed underneath Meg's window and out of sight, and then from inside the box came the clicking of claws on wood, the rustle and brush of scales against the walls, and finally, after a beat, the juicy rip of chicken. Meg slammed the lever down ...

Now, it's your turn. Take a challenge, if you will. It will

pay off. Make lists of what you learn from Komodo dragon Jata's entrance to the book: 1) appearance and body texture; 2) physical actions and how they are performed, e.g., speed of each action; 3) modes of perception; 4) motivation; 5) anything else. How many items did you find? Quite a few, I suspect. Think about how Mejia structured the scene to accomplish that much. The passage is a course in itself, and the process can be applied to the books you read.

And so we get to resources for developing the reality of your character: ways to learn about your animal or animals in your opus, whether it's your magnum opus of Animalia or the also-ran characters in a work centered elsewhere. If you're not already a specialist or keen observer of the animal in question—say, again, your animal is a bear—it's time to hit the stacks and (you know) the Internet.

I suggest that you organize your research from the broad and basic side down. (Hint: a search term like "bear animal" avoids hits like a pileup of Chicago Bears.) Many sites and animal books are organized with a general introduction to the family or genus so they don't have to repeat information common to the group, information you might otherwise miss. You will also learn the scientific name of your target species, and that gives you an additional Internet search term, somewhat more stable than regionally variable common names. The scientific name is especially useful for more academic sources. As always, take care to assess the trustworthiness of a site for the type of information you're after.

Wikipedia gives you a good start to get a general understanding of common characteristics of the family— *Ursidae* for the bears—often extended articles, links to the species level, and selected literature. In this case, too, the Wikipedia article tells you that there are two species known as "black bear," American and European. Not knowing that, it would be easy to be misled by British publications.

Decent public libraries have books and videos devoted to animals overall and about many individual species. Even those big coffee-table animal books and some children's books are good for photo study. And, of course, your reference librarians, college/university libraries, interlibrary loan, and the libraries' databases are your best friends.

If you're writing about other best friends—a dog, cat, horse, bird, or other well-studied species, the behavioral bibliography is immense. Think piles of books on canine intelligence and communication. Common and nearby species promise more opportunity at direct observations than rare species. I think of Luis Baptista, who made major contributions by studying the different songs of the common white-crowned sparrows on either side of the Golden Gate Bridge and other accessible parts of his region.

If you're writing about a rarely seen and studied species, you may face the opposite problem from dog lit: not enough information. Animal behavior departments discourage student field studies of animals that are uncommon or difficult to access because a thesis will never be forthcoming if the student sees few or no individuals. I know of a graduate group in Britain that was taken to East Africa to do a population study of pancake tortoises. They found none. If you are considering a species rare enough to be threatened or endangered, you will probably have to be content without fieldwork, but many of those special species have received plenty of attention in print and video.

Searching for academic papers in Google Scholar (right at hand) and other technical databases via a library card may dig out information you can use. Many scientific journals and databases of journals charge for online access to papers, but abstracts are normally available without cost. Public universities can sometimes offer their databases to the public if they work onsite, and they typically have huge holdings in animal studies, especially if they maintain a veterinary school or lean toward the study of whole animals. Harder to find are individual chapters of multi-author books, which may not be described by chapter in library listings. Relevant chapters can be buried in academic anthologies or papers or abstracts from conferences. Here, again, ask your reference librarians.

Then read and read and watch documentaries about your target species, noting characteristics of body and behavior that you'll be able to draw on as you create details of your real, somewhat real, or wholly invented character. The PBS *Nature* series, especially the recent programs with their extraordinary scientific and technical expertise, is excellent, and you can track programs on Amazon to stream. Recent programs are online, and some may be available at libraries. You can find old ones in collections to buy on VHS for next to nothing. Pause and slow motion will help you sketch and write notes from the videos.

Remember that nonhuman animals, like us, have differences in behavior between ages, sexes, and the combinations thereof. (Dominance, fighting, courting ... who needs guns for drama?) Once you have a good understanding of the normal behavior of the species, be aware that, also like us, animals have individual differences. For example, nearly everyone I meet asks if turtles have personalities. The answer? Yes, they do. I notice a wide range in personality, interests, and skills: in personality, from retiring and laid-back to "Type A" assertiveness, intensity, and impatience, even within species.

If you have access to individuals of the target species, all the better. For some animals, travel and field study is ideal but often not practical, and we must rely on the voices of others. Ask the experts, and read accounts by keen watchers. For some, seek out the pets, the neighbor's llamas, the zoo, a primate research center, preserved animals at a museum or nature center, the bears at the garbage containers.

I mention the garbage containers because that's the way I watched wild bears. This non-artist was taking a biological illustration class in California's Sierras. One evening our instructor took us to a tiny nearby town that collected community garbage for pickup in large, open-top drop boxes. The bears came every night, and, from a safe distance near the cars, we filled page after page with quick outlines of bears' postures in, on, and out of the containers. If I hadn't been in a drawing class or if the bears had sat still for a moment, I could have been writing behavioral notes, but sketching is useful, too—postures to remind you to describe. Those Dumpster-dipping bears stood partway along a line from wholly wild to imprinted, captive, or domesticated, and even those categories break down depending on the degree of relationship to people, with huge differences in behavior along and around that highly generalized line. If in your memoir you're remembering the circus bear cub riding a bicycle, your model is far different from a wild bear. Wild behavior is the starting point, but long domestication and individual circumstances change behavior of individuals and even of groups.

In Brian Doyle's *Martin Marten*, a man of the woods gives young Dave—and us—some good advice about field observation.

What say we go for a couple of hours now as quietly as we can and keep our eyes peeled, this time for animals and their habits and customs and trails and territories. Animals live in certain ways, and when you pay close attention to their ways, what they like, what they are most comfortable with, that's when you go down a few layers deeper ... There's always something new that the books and Web sites and grizzled old veterans of the woods don't know.

Watch. Remember affection, absorption, intraspecies relationships. Capture images by pencil, camera, or video. Write it down. It's like overhearing a conversation on the bus and borrowing from the dialogue. It's a writing course, a treasure trove of detail. I know that if I hadn't recorded behaviors in my lab for decades, I would never be able to write my nonfiction book, yet I wish for even deeper detail.

Ernest Thompson Seton, a naturalist writing in the first half of the twentieth century and known for his precise descriptions of wild animals, was one of the keen observers. He once gave the also-famous William Beebe, about to leave for a two-year research trip, a piece of advice. Seton wrote:

> There will come a time, say in the heart of Borneo, when you think you have exhausted your study and observations of some particular area or subject, and will look around at a loss to add any more notes. Instantly close your eyes tight, and keep them closed for several minutes, while you tell yourself in a most convincing manner that you are now back in your laboratory in New York, never to return to Borneo again. Ask yourself if there is anything you wish you had noticed, or

watched, or collected, or photographed. Five minutes of this self-questioning, this egocentric third degree, will always materialize a crop of the most common, apparent things or phenomena which you had overlooked, to which you should have paid special attention and didn't.

Later, Beebe said he'd tried Seton's technique "scores of times and invariably my eyes pop open and I begin renewed, enthusiastic investigation … [I]t is a real spur to jaded eyes and mind."

An important point: Please, please, don't dumb your animals down. They don't have to be total deadheads or, for that matter, speak at conferences like Tawada's mama polar bear. There is so much research popping up about intelligence in animals, including brain plasticity, bringing new respect even to tiny-brained animals whose brains aren't organized like ours, that real animals can fascinate us from their own minds. The days of animal automatons and chains of reflexes are over. Look for evidence of learning, teaching, decision-making, creativity, novelty. A favorite quote of mine is a *New York Times* headline and jump head about the newly named field of "coldblooded cognition": "COLDBLOODED DOES NOT MEAN STUPID: Coldblooded, but Surprisingly Smart." Love is one thing that drives people to save species. Identity and respect, especially for "smart" animals, are the others.

Still, we must remember that even if some animals seem nothing like us and are difficult to understand, each species has what it needs to live in its place—often things we can't do—and deserves a place of its own, respect, and a part of our hearts. Penelope Scambly Schott's "Among the Other Animals" hangs on my wall and is often read.

Among the Other Animals
Please excuse me as I carry this leg-waving beetle
out to the yard and watch it go.

Surely it values its walking to and fro upon the
earth
as I value my own.

Sometimes I envy the salmon who knows how
to go
back to the river in which it hatched.

I have been at sea a long time and am sniffing
my way home. This is the estuary

where the text of selfhood is not words or tools
nor any ability to anticipate death.

Nights when I answer the screech owl, music
vibrates
the back of my throat,

a language half known: a Spanish speaker almost
understanding Portuguese,

until I become one in the common clan of beasts,
the animal itself, akin to kin.

Finally, read and study the masters of writing about and for
animals, such as this piece of writerly inspiration: a selection
from the end of the osprey essay in Finn's *Wild Delicate Seconds*.

When the osprey rises it turns the fish forward, torpedo-wise, and flies off in the direction of the setting sun—victory clenched in its talons. The fish struggles in the burning air, tail fin waving like a broken rudder, and the osprey gives a shivering, shimmering, ghostly air-dance, water shed in all directions.

Bird-fish-sky-water. Life-death-hunger-desire. You can have your movies. You can have your TV.

Works Cited

Beebe, William. 1944. Introduction to Ernest Thompson Seton's "The Sea Otter." In *The Book of Naturalists: An anthology of the best natural history*, edited by William Beebe. New York: Alfred A. Knopf.

Childs, Craig. 2007. *The Animal Dialogues: Uncommon Encounters in the Wild*. New York: Little, Brown, and Company.

Doyle, Brian. 2015. *Martin Marten*. New York: Thomas Dunne Books/St. Martin's Press.

Finn, Charles. 2012. *Wild Delicate Seconds: 29 Wildlife Encounters*. Corvallis, OR: Oregon State University Press.

Gilbert, William S., music by Arthur Sullivan. 1885. Libretto for *The Mikado, or The Town of Titipu*.

Gould, Stephen Jay. 1993. *Eight Little Piggies: Reflections in Natural History*. New York: W. W. Norton & Company.

Kerasote, Ted. 2007. *Merle's Door: Lessons from a Freethinking Dog*. Orlando, FL: Harcourt, Inc.

Lombard, Rosemary Douglas. 2016. *Turtles All the Way: Poems*. Georgetown, KY: Finishing Line Press.

Mejia, Mindy. 2012. *The Dragon Keeper*. Ashland, OR: Ashland Creek Press.

Moore, Kathleen Dean. 1999. *Holdfast: At Home in the Natural World*. New York: The Lyons Press.

———. 2016. *Piano Tide*. Berkeley, CA: Counterpoint Press.

Pyle, Robert Michael. 2018. *Magdalena Mountain*. Berkeley, CA: Counterpoint Press.

———. 2000. *Walking the High Ridge: Life as Field Trip*. Minneapolis, MN: Milkweed Editions.

Ryder, Joanne. 1987. *Chipmunk Song*. Illustrated by Lynne Cherry. New York: Lodestar/Dutton/Penguin Books USA.

Schott, Penelope Scambly. 2010. "Among the Other Animals." *Six Lips*. Bay City, MI: Maypole Press.

Seton, Ernest Thompson. 1944. Letter to William Beebe quoted by Beebe in his introduction to Seton's "The Sea Otter." *The Book of Naturalists: An Anthology of the Best Natural History*. New York: Alfred A. Knopf.

Tawada, Yoko. 2016. *Memoirs of a Polar Bear*. Translated by Susan Bernofsky. New York: New Directions Books.

Part II:
The Craft of Writing about Animals

Meeting the Wild Things Where They Are

Kipp Wessel

Trace our life forms back far enough, our segregated cluster of genomes and basal cells, and we are gilled beings moving slowly through inky water, our webbed appendages, short of skill to pull ourselves to shore, dangling limp at our sides. Suspended in our liquid world, we stare at the moon, comforted by its familiar round shape, its glow through the haze. We fill our simple stomachs with enough matter to quiet the want, and we shut our eyes, again, to darkness.

This is who we are. From this, we came—all of us did. If you start at the beginning, it's less of a leap to crawl inside the skin of another species. We, ourselves, have known the world from that evolving epidermis multiple times over.

When writing about the lives of animals, we need to remind ourselves there's less that separates than joins us. Start there. At our core, we're in this together. And from there, we can imagine the world through their eyes. Go there.

As a fiction writer, the pull to incorporate wilderness and animal lives into my own work is a constant. Animals hold my personal interest, but I also realize the depth of texture, intrigue, and dramatic tension they can immediately fill within the stories I create, a part of the integral tableau of human experience. For it's the forces larger, louder, and stranger than we are that mesmerize us. The muddy path of the unpredictable, the raging storm when it swallows the sky. Wild things, including those within us, capture our gazes, lead us on, and beg us to round the corner in pursuit of their wet imprint across dark sod.

Wilderness and animal lives tap a vibrant currency within our writing due to their simultaneous proximity and mystery within our shared world. Forget about aliens making contact from distant galaxies. Foreign species already share our window wells and dewed lawns. When we choose to include them in our writing, and when we get them right, we capture lightning in a bottle—vibrant life force and all its current, momentarily suspended.

But I'm a writer who would argue that the getting them right part, when it comes to animal lives in our literature, is a practice more often tried than accomplished. Bottled lightning is a messy practice. It's hard to capture a force of nature—all those charged ion particles racing in opposite directions—by instinct alone. More often than not, we settle for a close approximation, singular representations that can pass for the real thing—if you don't look too closely, if we can bank on shared assumptions.

I'm not sure why we refrain from delving deeper, below the surface, when it comes to writing animal lives. Some do. But so many of us stop short. We leave out the most important element—the one that breathes the deepest, loudest life within its being. We focus on biology, at best, and false narratives, at worst, but more often than not, we leave out the animal's soul. Or worse, forget it has one. And when we neglect that essential element, we end up with all bottle, no lightning. Think of James Audubon's countless drawings of avian subjects—each one perfectly rendered, each one perfectly lifeless.

What if we chose to move closer? How would our work benefit from a better understanding of the foreign species we share our world with? My personal role model for this practice isn't a writer or artist at all but an explorer of oceans—a deep sea diver named Cousteau—the French inventor of the aqua lung who donned a red knit watch cap and dove the sea with his anvil nose leading the way. Cousteau had the right idea: If you want to capture something wild, don't capture it at all— that's the single most important key. Meet it where it is, on its terms (not yours). Follow it. Learn not just its behaviors and bend of vertebrae, but also its character, its unique essence, it's soul. *That's* the stuff that matters and charges our writing with energy. Cousteau got that right nearly every time he scrunched his scuba mask across his face and sunk his body into the saline world beneath him. He let the power of the camera lens and his endlessly curious mind capture the foreign life forms that swim beneath us, his own presence in the process an invisible witness, his own being weightless.

Animals, whether bounding through the backyard sumac or the Serengeti, are as dimensional as their human neighbors. Those of us who share our homes with them already know this truth. A dog is not a dog. A dog is. A barn owl is. An aardvark is. Animals are as sentient and multifaceted as any human being (sometimes more so). We need to be reminded of this when we delve into the writing of animal lives within the stories we tell. Regardless of nostrils or gills, those who have two feet or twenty, many vertebrae or none—each animal, bird, and reptile of the world has a life force and personality all its own.

A friend of mine studied the behavior of snails as part of a two-year study at Lake Tanganyika. When I asked her if the lives of common mollusks warranted the intensive study at hand, she detailed, at length, the individual behavior traits, practically the full breadth of the Myers-Briggs personality inventory, across her sluggish subjects.

A snail is.

Collective behaviors and individual nuances co-exist across all lives of all species. That truth widens the writer's aperture of possibility as much as it does his or her responsibility to grant it the justice of authenticity when we choose to breathe foreign beings to life in our work. When writing about wild things, proximity matters. We must get as close as we possibly can to who and what they are. See them. Know them. And for a moment (or more), become them.

When I began drafting my first novel, it became quickly obvious that bears (North American black and grizzlies) would hold a central place within the storyline. The novel was about a young man who loses a brother, begins to lose his first love, and becomes obsessed with wild bears to the point he wants to become one of them. Drawn from my own experience of loss and grief, I gravitated to bears and their ability to hibernate whole seasons as a potentially rich subtext for the vortex of clinical depression in which my main character finds himself.

In the novel, bears are subverted and inverted. They hold a real place within the storyline and a symbolic one within the character's imagination. Both forms had to be real—truthful (the authentic and the imagined). My first task was to mine the magnitude and electricity of the foreign nation known as "bear"—their biology, physiology, and behaviors. An entire length of wall in my writing room became a library of books on bears—every tome I could get my hands on, some two dozen volumes of the most recent, renowned scientific literature. One by one, I devoured these texts. Notes and highlight marks and Post-it markers threaded each one. Pretty soon, I was immersed in the tapestry of new possibilities.

Understanding liberates our imaginations. With animals, it's rarely the other way around. The more we unravel, the wider our field of vision. When we are fully satiated with what "bear is," then we can embark on the artist's role of creative reconstruction. We take pieces of truth and weave them with the glutton of imagination. We let the light pass through, and these fragments join to piece our story. And our art.

Writing about lives with survival behaviors, belief systems, and adaptations we can mostly only guess at is an experiment of hope, followed by hard work. To embark on the path of writing about wild things requires a Donald Rumsfeld embrace of the unknown knowns and known unknowns, with the want and luck to land somewhere in between.

And yet. For a fiction writer, that's also the infinite draw. The secret lives of field mice, when explored, can inspire and help create a wide landscape of new possibility. Tamping the roots of wild things in our stories has a unique literary power—one that can simultaneously ground the reader in the world and open up whole new universes, formally unexplored, right in our own backyards.

There's an inverse law in the creative process—the more you know and understand, the more you can make up. Art isn't the liberation of truth. More so is the opposite relation. Truth fuels the liberation that widens art.

The natural world provides an endless tableau for the

fiction writer to explore and lift the grains of its wonder to the surface, posit fragments of authentic and literal truths, layer by layer, not just to ground our characters and stories but to transform them. In our fiction, in our art, wild things are sacred gods. We have to get them as right as we possibly can—not just to help educate others about what the world is, what it is made of, and the web that surrounds us—but also to help keep the work itself as vibrant as possible as time moves past its release into the world. We owe the world; we owe our work.

How much did Jack London get right about wolves? Melville and his whale? Hemingway and his marlin? Because wherever we miss authenticity of representation, wherever we rely on our imaginations more than our field observations or research to authenticate the flora and fauna we center in our work, we risk subverting the authenticity of every other layer of all other forms of truth we are attempting to capture, and the art of our work itself.

Research is imperative. But so is the more obtuse task of unearthing the radically different experience of animal lives from our own. Write about the backyard salamander, but after you've imagined yourself in its permeable skin and larval world. Imagine the capability to regrow whole limbs, your sole tool for dining an extended, sticky tongue. Take a full Kafka one-way ticket into the metamorphosis of the animal you hope to present to the world. And then poke your snout through the soil and tell us what you see.

Somewhere between the task of getting angels to dance on the end of the pin and the full bottle capture of electric particles charging the clouds is how it works. Part Art, part Science, and the remaining part Belief. And part of it, too, has to be the act of Forgetting. I imagine Cousteau did that each time he lowered himself from the bridge of *Calypso*, cleared his mind of all his preconceptions as his rubber-finned feet immersed into sea, his imagination fully open to whatever new discovery awaited him, the entire ocean, all 300 million cubic miles of seafloor a clean slate, an opening of wonder each time he merged into its being.

Easier said than done, bottled lighting and angels posed on pins. But imagine the endless lives and possibilities in the woods and fields surrounding us, and the rewards waiting as we move our pens and eyes and imaginations closer to their worlds.

A few years ago I built a small studio, two feet from the soil, lodged between three oaks overlooking the lakeshore near my home. I enclosed the space for shelter against the weather but filled the walls with operable windows for a 270-degree view. Unlike most writing spaces that work to quiet the world, I wanted mine to be an open window to it. It is my terrestrial version of Cousteau's diving bell.

In my tiny studio, I listen to the wind rush through the reeds, the mallards land on the current, the trumpeter swans warble as they pass overhead. I watch their shadows cross the winnowed lake surface, the murmuration of swallows and starlings wash into the distance. As I write this now, two young deer are moving through the dead cattails along the shoreline, their eight deer feet in the cold water of early winter, snow-covered muskrat mounds behind their forms. I watch the two deer snouts nudge the dried stalks, their four ears twitch in every possible direction. Though I am but twenty feet away, neither of the deer notice my presence. And for this moment, I am immersed in their world. Theirs, not mine.

When we merge into the sanctuary and separate peace of wilderness, lose ourselves in its cadence, writing comes easily. Our thoughts drift its gentle current; we are reminded of its largess and grace. The artist's role is to lift that wonder to the surface. And to do that, you have to first know it at a distance of the cowl of its breath. And soul.

Rewilding Literature: Catalyzing Compassion for Wild Predators through Creative Nonfiction

Paula MacKay

As I write, wolves in Washington are once again making front-page news. A young wolf from the so-called Huckleberry pack was gunned down from a helicopter, with the wolf's shooter contracted by the state to remove up to four wolves in response to sheep depredations on leased grazing land. Conservationists are angry that, for the second time in two years, wolves in this region are dying because they're behaving like wolves in wolf country. Agency spokespersons defend their actions by arguing that the Huckleberry pack poses an ongoing threat to livestock.

When my husband and I moved to the Pacific Northwest eight years ago to study large carnivores, wolves were iconic ghosts of a wilder past, having been exterminated from Washington by the 1930s. But not long after our arrival, the unexpected happened. Wildlife biologists discovered an active wolf den within state boundaries, from which five wolf pups emerged like ambassadors of a lost era. Many people celebrated, and I was among them. I was also concerned. Wolves were being killed both legally and illegally in the Northern Rockies, only a few years after they were famously reintroduced to Yellowstone National Park. I hoped things might play out differently here given that Washington is a mecca for wildlife enthusiasts. Now I'm not so sure.

For much of my adulthood, I have struggled with how to best use my writing skills to benefit wildlife, especially in controversial situations like the one surrounding wolves. In my work as a conservationist and a field biologist, I could compose an op-ed expressing my view that wolves who kill sheep are not criminals, and that it is we humans who must reform our ways if we want wildness (and people) to thrive in the future. I could co-author a scientific article summarizing how wolves and other apex predators help to regulate natural communities, or I could develop a brochure explaining their ecological role to a broader audience. I could draft a grant proposal seeking funding for pertinent studies, edit a book of research methodologies for fellow field biologists, or create a website with graphics and pretty pictures. The problem is, I've already done all this in my career—many others have done all this and more. Yet wolves are still being shot from helicopters.

In this paper, I will explore how writers of creative nonfiction can use their craft to foster empathy for wild predators and promote compassion on their behalf. More specifically, I'll examine how several notable authors have employed literary devices like figurative language, anthropomorphism, juxtaposition, and point of view to make scientific knowledge about predators more palatable and persuasive to readers.

Rewilding Our Hearts

We live in a time replete with information about biodiversity loss, climate change, and other environmental catastrophes. Scientists warn that half of the species existing today may be gone by the end of this century. Large mammalian predators are especially vulnerable to extinction because of their inherently low population densities, slow rates of reproduction, and susceptibility to persecution by people. We're also faced with overwhelming evidence that our own species is to blame for what has now been deemed the Earth's sixth mass extinction, putting us right up there with asteroids and volcanic eruptions in our capacity for global devastation.

Still, we continue to operate as though this potentially apocalyptic scenario pertains to a planet whose fate is not our own. Information overload no doubt plays a significant role in our lack of collective action; most of us can only take so much gloom and doom before turning to red wine and chocolate or Monday Night Football. Not long ago, I walked with hundreds of women, men, and children in downtown Seattle as part of a climate change march that rallied citizens worldwide. At the same time, more than 68,000 Seattle Seahawks fans set an attendance record at CenturyLink Field. Final score? Seahawks 1, Climate Change 0.

As we chanted past bustling restaurants and curious apartment dwellers peering down from their balconies, I reflected on what it would take to empty the football stands and fill the streets with people cheering for polar bears, wolverines, and the millions of human beings whose survival is threatened by our warming climate. More numbers? Bleaker projections? I know that good science is critical to gauging our ecological predicament and planning for the future, but after two-plus decades working in conservation, I've come to embrace that inundating people with data does not in itself enhance wisdom or transform behavior. In *Rewilding Our Hearts*, animal behaviorist Marc Bekoff writes:

> When we make decisions that damage the environment or harm animals, it is rarely because of a lack of knowledge and concrete data. Rather, losses to biodiversity, inadequate animal protections, and other negative impacts are typically due to problems of human psychology and social and cultural factors. Science alone doesn't hold the answers to the current crisis nor does it get people to feel compassion or to act differently.

As a pathway to saving species and reversing environmental destruction, Bekoff encourages his readers to deeply imagine the world from the perspective of wild beings and to act accordingly—to "rewild" their hearts and minds. He borrows *rewilding* from the field of conservation biology, which broadly defines the term as landscape-scale conservation aimed at maintaining core wilderness areas, reconnecting them via corridors of habitat, and restoring apex predators. Applying this concept to humans, Bekoff sees the process of rewilding as "a personal journey and transformative exploration that centers on bringing other animals and their homes, all ecosystems, back into our heart." Intuitively, rewilding counteracts unwilding, "the process by which we become alienated from nature and nonhuman animals." This distancing, Bekoff argues—a hazard of modern life—erodes our innate connection with wild nature and thus our willingness to defend it.

Few scientists outwardly share Bekoff's passion or sensibilities when it comes to animal welfare and its relationship to conservation. Among conservation biologists, however, he is hardly alone in emphasizing the role of human values in protecting wild predators. Carnivore ecologist Cristina Eisenberg expresses sentiments similar to Bekoff's in her book *The Carnivore Way*: "Science and environmental law can help us learn to share landscapes with fierce creatures, but ultimately, coexistence has to do with our human hearts." Peer-reviewed papers on this topic abound in the scientific literature, and the value-based challenges of coexisting with predators are frequently discussed at wildlife conferences and meetings.

Although predator conservation is widely recognized as a people problem, the goal of increasing human tolerance for wolves and other top-level carnivores is not easily accomplished. In some cases, financial incentives have been an effective tool for promoting nonlethal predator management and reducing poaching, though a scientific review conducted by Adrian Treves and Jeremy Bruskotter suggests that money doesn't buy tolerance in people who are heavily influenced by social factors fueling anti-predator values (e.g., peer group norms, government-sanctioned killing of predators).

A scientific cure for intolerance has yet to be discovered, but Bekoff's approach is more holistic than prescriptive. His overarching message is this: To truly care about the well-being of others—whether they travel on two legs or four, slither through muck or soar through the sky—requires imaginative empathy and an open heart. What would it be like to be a mother wolf being chased by a helicopter, or a hungry polar bear with no ice in sight? For that matter, how might it feel to be a third-generation rancher losing sheep to wolves, or a grief-stricken activist impassioned to speak for creatures with no voice?

Biologists are reluctant to anthropomorphize wildlife, citing the myriad mysteries of animal minds. Nonetheless, the line separating human and nonhuman behavior, once considered solid, has become fuzzier in recent times. Jeffrey Masson and Susan McCarthy described grief in elephants, for instance, and Jane Goodall documented intercommunity aggression in chimpanzees not unlike that exemplified by human warfare. Despite such valuable revelations, it is beyond the reach of science to fully comprehend the emotional lives and motivations of other species. But as Bekoff points out, this limitation in no way justifies our mistreatment of nonhuman animals.

"As a scientist," Bekoff writes, "I know that it's never enough to simply imagine another animal's perspective. But as a person, I know that it's never enough to accept unclarity or uncertainty about animal minds as a reason not to care for them, or as an excuse for inaction or willful harm." Bekoff further posits that our attitude about the otherness of animals is linked to our behavior toward fellow humans; indeed, human rights atrocities across the globe are a sobering reminder of what happens when perceived differences between "us" and "them" become grounds for abuse. Sociological research published by Kimberly Costello and Gordon Hodson demonstrates that devaluing animals because they are different from us actually predicts prejudice toward human outgroups (e.g., immigrants, other races).

It's Story Time

One of the great gifts of literature is that it allows us to inhabit the stories of others and acquire new insights. Literary scholar Suzanne Keen contends that reading promotes narrative empathy—vicarious feelings and perspective induced by narratives about another. During times of crisis, insights derived from narrative empathy might even help nudge us toward pivotal change.

In her essay "Creative Responses to Worlds Unraveling: The Artist in the 21st Century," author Ann Pancake—whose political novel, *Strange As This Weather Has Been*, unearthed the ecological and social evils of mountaintop removal in Appalachia—explores how writers can help kindle compassion in readers who have become desensitized to global trauma and cataclysmic forecasts:

> I believe literature is one of the most powerful antidotes we have to "psychic numbing." It's not easy to actually feel, with our hearts, with our guts, overwhelming abstract problems that don't directly affect us, especially now, with so many catastrophes unfolding around us, and it's tough to sustain compassion for the nameless souls struggling with those catastrophes. But we do have great capacity to empathize with the personal stories of individuals.

Pancake suggests that, unlike journalism—and, I would add, science writing—creative writing tends to reveal the interior lives of its characters. "If the writer can evoke these interior lives with complexity and compassion," Pancake continues, "the reader's understanding of social injustice and environmental disaster is dramatically broadened and deepened." This task obviously becomes all the more challenging when crafting stories about nonhuman animals, whose interior lives are available to us only through projection and speculation. Such stories are thus prone to sentimentality on one end of the spectrum and emotional detachment on the other.

Many works of fiction, especially children's fiction, evoke empathy for animals by telling the story from their imagined point of view. Popular examples range from classics like E. B. White's *Charlotte's Web* and Jack London's *Call of the Wild* to Garth Stein's more contemporary *The Art of Racing in the Rain* and Barbara Gowdy's *The White Bone*. But how does one convey the perspective of spiders or dogs or elephants in nonfiction in a way that is moving, believable, and true? To further up the ante, how can nonfiction literature help tame the lions, tigers, and bears of our imagination and rouse compassion for wildlife generally presumed to be dangerous to humans?

Natural history and other scientific background is key to demystifying wild predators and debunking myths about the risk they pose to people; my shelves overflow with technical books whose well-researched content has the potential to defuse most anti-predator rhetoric—if only facts possessed such persuasive powers. But the societal shift needed to cultivate a more peaceful coexistence with predators and to rescue them from the dark corners of our subconscious demands that we both learn about and *become awakened to* the many forms of life with which we share the Earth.

For too long, storytelling has exploited human fear and misunderstanding of wild predators at their ultimate expense—a legacy perpetuated in today's popular media. Global threats to large carnivores call for a new body of literature that encourages respect for these animals versus vilification and

96

widespread persecution. As Jack Turner puts it in *The Abstract Wild*: "The necessary work of science produces information, but what we need are stories, stories that produce love."

The Tiger

By combining scientific information and storytelling techniques borrowed from fiction, creative nonfiction writers have the potential to draw readers into the unfamiliar and perhaps uncomfortable emotional territory necessary to rewild our hearts and minds. As with fiction, gripping material is helpful; Suzanne Keen cites research showing that readers are physiologically aroused when characters are involved in a suspenseful situation. John Vaillant's 2010 bestseller, *The Tiger*, for example, thrusts readers into a crushing narrative about a man-eating tiger in the Russian Far East, which in turn acts as a portal to the complex dynamics of poaching, politics, and illegal trade that threaten tigers worldwide.

Catalyzing empathy for any wildlife is problematic enough, but to do so for animals capable of eating us is especially difficult. Written with the flair of a murder mystery, Vaillant's book could have easily characterized the tiger as a psychopathic killer undeserving of ethical consideration or species-level protection. Alternately, a story told from the perspective of the starving tiger might have trivialized the human issues relevant to their conservation.

So how does Vaillant awaken his readers to the plight of an animal preying on poverty-stricken people in post-Perestroika Siberia? He goes to great lengths to illustrate the socio-political, cultural, and ecological factors underlying the tragic conflict around which the story unfolds. Through his dialogue with villagers, wildlife investigators, and others, Vaillant reveals that this particular tiger has been reduced to stalking people because his human-induced injuries preclude him from successfully hunting anything else. Once we learn that the man-eating tiger "had been shot an extraordinary number of times" and that "this tiger had absorbed bullets the way Moby-Dick absorbed harpoons," we come to better understand, if not condone, his killing of humans for food. Concludes the investigator in charge of the case: "It was men who were responsible for the aggression of this animal."

Many of the villagers co-inhabiting the tiger's territory, including his first victim, have resorted to poaching wildlife for lack of other economic opportunities. Vaillant doesn't refrain from describing the threat tigers can pose to people—this threat is obviously central to his story. But by juxtaposing the hardships experienced by tigers with those of the marginalized human communities dependent on the same landscapes and resources, we come to empathize with the wild predators as well as the people. The author shows us that all the characters in his story, humans and nonhumans alike, are trying to eke out a living in a harsh environment, and that their well-being is intimately connected. At times, Vaillant explicitly compares tigers and humans to stimulate further empathy for the former:

> Both of us demand large territories; both of us have prodigious appetites for meat; both of us require control over our living space and are prepared to defend it, and both of us have an enormous sense of entitlement to the resources around us. If a tiger can poach on another's territory, it probably will, and so, of course, will we. A key difference, however, is that tigers take only what they need.

Here, Vaillant counters the stereotypical image of tigers as killing machines, emphasizing that it is humans who are actually guilty of taking more than we need to survive. Although Vaillant effectively employs juxtaposition and other literary techniques to engage readers in the wild predator's point of view, some readers (especially scientists) may find his imaginative prose overly anthropomorphic at times. Consider his premise that the man-eating tiger was actively seeking revenge on poachers:

> The Amur tiger's territoriality and capacity for sustained vengeance, for lack of a better word, are the stuff of both legend and fact. What is amazing—and also terrifying about tigers— is their facility for what can only be described as abstract thinking. Very quickly, a tiger can assimilate new information—evidence, if you will—ascribe it to a source, and even a motive, and react accordingly.

Given that we cannot know how the tiger perceives his victims, to attribute his actions to vengeance seems a gratuitous leap. Regardless, it is a testament to Vaillant's skill as a writer that even skeptics will question their assumptions about the tiger's ability to think and feel. Through his well-crafted story, the author helps elucidate the extent to which we are jeopardizing the future of tigers—and ourselves.

Would a cautionary tale about poaching be nearly as compelling if another imperiled animal took center stage— the leatherback turtle, say, or the little-known pangolin (a burrowing mammal whose overlapping scales have been likened to the leaves of an artichoke)? It certainly could, depending on the storyteller; Susan Orlean penned a bestseller about the illegal collection of rare orchids. But given our innate fascination with predators, they serve as especially potent fodder for creative nonfiction. One need only read the editorial pages about wolves to recognize that large, meat-eating animals possess a unique and paradoxical charisma that renders them at once alluring and odious. Throughout history, predators have been objects of both veneration and loathing in human culture.

Monster of God

Science writer David Quammen explores this paradox in his meticulously researched book *Monster of God*, for which he traveled to several remote areas of the world where humans still have a perilously intimate relationship with native large carnivores (e.g., Asiatic lions in India's Gir Forest, brown bears in Romania's Carpathian Mountains). Quammen proposes that wild predators historically provided us with stories of both heroism and humility, thus helping us to define our place in nature: "For as long as *Homo sapiens* has been sapient—for much longer if you count the evolutionary wisdom stored in our genes—alpha predators have kept us acutely aware of our membership with the natural world." How? "They've done it by reminding us that to them we're just another flavor of meat."

Not surprisingly, Quammen argues, those big-bodied predators sometimes characterized as "man-eaters" (e.g., tigers, brown bears, great white sharks) occupy an especially dark and prominent place in the human mind, with the very term itself commemorating "an elemental experience—the experience in which, on rare occasions, members of our own species are relegated to the status of edible meat." Further, he postulates, although fear of death obviously looms large, the idea of actually *being consumed* pushes predators into a category of horror all their own.

"The extra dimension of dread," Quammen writes, "derives largely from ancient concerns about funerary observances and the deceased's prospects in an afterlife. Respectful, decorous disposal of the mortal remains has been important across virtually all times and cultures." I concur with Quammen's theory, as it seems that most humans hold a strong aversion to the desecration of dead bodies. I can't help but wonder, in fact, if this notion of desecration also plays a role in the venomous reaction some people have to livestock depredation by wild carnivores—especially given that livestock are typically destined for the slaughterhouse (where dismemberment occurs behind thick concrete walls). Once, while I was wolf-watching in Yellowstone National Park, a fellow observer turned to me and unabashedly confessed his hatred of wolves. His reason? Because they killed some of his friend's sheep and chewed away their "butts." The man appeared to be much more upset about the sheep's desecration than their untimely deaths.

History, mythology, and prejudices aside, wild predators pose little risk to modern humanity, and man-eaters are notably rare. Fortunately, there are many stories worth telling about these intriguing animals that don't revolve around their consuming people, and creative nonfiction can help make these stories inspirational to the reader.

In her essay cited above, Pancake reminds us "...the transformative properties of literature are not limited to its content. Literature's form, too—its style, structure, figures of speech, tone, mood, formal originality, and experimentation— evoke in readers fresh and profound understandings." Some of the most influential books I've read about predators are effective primarily because they make masterful use of such elements, with predation being almost incidental to the author's exploration of form and his or her own interior world. In other words, the author's story is projected through his or her experience with predators as much as the predator's story is projected through the author. By the end of the narrative, it is usually the author, not the predator, who is transformed.

A Sand County Almanac

Aldo Leopold's *A Sand County Almanac* provides a classic example of transformation. One of the most influential conservation thinkers of the twentieth century, Leopold is considered by many to be the father of wildlife management. He came into his early career at a time when few questioned the ethics of killing predators, including Leopold himself. In *A Sand County Almanac*, the author weaves together personal narrative and exposition to convey the evolution of his perspective as a scientist and a passionate advocate for nature.

For purposes of organization, the book is divided into three sections of essays: Part I: A Sand County Almanac; Part II: Sketches Here and There; and Part III: The Upshot.

In his foreword, Leopold describes these sections as: Part I, a collection of seasonal observations from his family's farm in Wisconsin; Part II, reflections on key episodes influencing his identity as a conservationist; and Part III, philosophical questions pertaining to how we should proceed in our relationship with the land and its wild inhabitants. Although each section stands alone in terms of tone and style, the sum becomes greater than its parts because Leopold invites us into the personal journey that led him to his ponderings in Part III. If he hadn't earned our allegiance to both him and the wildness he loves through the descriptive and narrative prose comprising Parts I and II, he might have lost us with the more polemical material presented in Part III. But by "The Upshot," we're convinced: We need to *do* something to save those honking geese, those dancing woodcocks ... that dying wolf.

Anyone attuned to environmentalism, even one who hasn't read Leopold's work, is likely familiar with his elegy for a dying wolf. "Thinking Like a Mountain" appears roughly halfway through the book, in the sketches dedicated to Arizona and New Mexico. Leopold begins this essay by arguing for the unique element of mystery with which wolves infuse the landscape—a mystery felt by virtually all who encounter wolf country ("only the ineducable tyro can fail to sense the presence or absence of wolves") but fully comprehended by none but the land itself ("only the mountain has lived long enough to listen objectively to the howl of the wolf").

Leopold goes on to tell us about his own epiphany regarding wolves, which, according to historians, occurred in 1909 in eastern Arizona's Apache National Forest. Leopold recalls that he and a companion were eating lunch by a river (later identified as the Black River) when they noticed a female wolf returning to her pups. The men impulsively opened fire, and Leopold notes that "when our rifles were empty, the old wolf was down, and a pup was dragging a leg into impassible slide-rocks." Already, we're empathizing with the injured wolves through the eyes of a reformed wolf killer, whose diction betrays that he no longer views them as varmints but rather a family broken by violence. It is the next passage, however, whose tone of redemption has reverberated through generations of environmentalists and others who care about wildlife:

We reached the old wolf in time to watch a fierce green fire dying in her eyes. I realized then, and have known ever since, that there was something new to me in those eyes—something known only to her and to the mountain. I was young then, and full of trigger itch; I thought that because fewer wolves meant more deer, that no wolves would mean hunters' paradise. But after seeing the green fire die, I sensed that neither the wolf nor the mountain agreed with such a view.

Typing these words of lament into my laptop, I felt a tremendous emotional blow—even after reading them so many times over the years, and knowing full well that Leopold's more enlightened attitude toward wolves realistically took decades to evolve. Why, then, is this scene so powerful to me and to millions of other readers? Because Leopold *metaphorically* captures the moment when his heart was rewilded, and restores our faith that such a transformation is possible. He also connects his audience with the predator's point of view. Here again is Pancake:

> Artists are also translators between the visible and invisible worlds, intermediaries between the profane and the sacred ... Literature re-sacralizes by illuminating the profound within the apparently mundane, by restoring reverence and wonder for the everyday, and by heightening our attentiveness and enlarging our compassion.

If Leopold had limited himself to scientific prose, he likely wouldn't have been able to serve as an intermediary between the profane (killing a mother wolf) and the sacred (wild nature). Instead, he chose to engage in what Bekoff calls "deep ethology," a practice in which the seer tries to imagine him or herself as the seen. By "thinking like a mountain" and seeing himself through the eyes of the dying wolf, Leopold was able to inspire compassion and reverence for a culturally maligned species and for the land itself. I'd venture to say that Leopold also became a better scientist as a result of this practice, capable of exploring visionary ecological ideas like those he put forth in Part III (e.g., "The Land Ethic," "Wilderness"). Bekoff points out that deep ethology is not simply an exercise in ethics but that "these intuitions can sometimes be the fodder for further scientific research and lead to verifiable information, to knowledge."

As demonstrated by Leopold and a growing number of writers, the merging of scientific exploration and personal exploration is a pillar of creative nonfiction focused on predators and other wildlife. Authors who share their inner process to this end help readers probe their own deeply held beliefs about wild nature.

Into Great Silence

In the prologue to her memoir *Into Great Silence*, orca biologist Eva Saulitis refers to a transformation like the one depicted in Leopold's green fire essay as an "origin moment"—a phrase she attributes to nature writer Susan Cerulean. Saulitis describes an origin moment as a profound experience in which one's perspective is dramatically altered, one's "assumptions about the world overturned." It becomes evident in the book that such experiences served to challenge her training in objectivity and sparked her imagination as an artist.

Saulitis's story of discovery is both intensely personal and profoundly ecological. The memoir centers on a catastrophic oil spill that devastated wildlife populations in south-central Alaska, as well as many human communities that were tied to them. Just after midnight on March 24, 1989, the infamous *Exxon Valdez* ran aground and dumped eleven million gallons of crude oil into Prince William Sound. More than twenty years later, Saulitis retells this tragic tale through the filter of her own experience as a field biologist studying orcas in the area. With the well-publicized particulars of the spill considered old news, she strives to move her readers in a fresh and visceral way. Here, Saulitis recounts her feelings of helplessness in the wake of the spill, when she was only twenty-five years old: "No matter what, the oil will pour from the ship's breached holds. The oil will spread. It will coat rocks and barnacles and kelp and otters and harbor seals and birds. It will kill orcas. It will change everything I know, everything I love."

And that it did. According to the *Exxon Valdez* Oil Spill Trustee Council, the spill ultimately fouled 1,300 miles of coastline, killing billions of fish and an estimated 250,000 seabirds; 2,800 sea otters; 300 harbor seals; 250 bald eagles; and 22 orcas. Saulitis renders these unfathomable numbers real by intertwining her own story as a woman with breast cancer with that of the wild predators she observes (Saulitis died of breast cancer in 2016). The result is part celebratory, part elegy—an inspiring marriage of scientific inquiry and heartfelt reflection.

Saulitis's elegant prose brings the place and its vivid characters, both human and wild, to life. Over the course of her book, we not only get to know Saulitis and her fellow researchers as real people with human flaws, but we develop relationships with killer whales who are, notably, given names: Eyak, Eccles, Ripple Fin. Their naming reflects distinct physical attributes—fin shapes, scratches, and other scars—that allow orca experts like Saulitis to tell them apart. Through her intimate observations of orca behavior, we come to see the orcas as individuals—mysterious yet familiar, wild but not totally free given the dire circumstances of the oil spill. We learn, too, that each pod (a group of related whales traveling together) has a unique dialect of calls, further allowing Saulitis and her readers to identify with these magnificent mammals of the sea. And to mourn their deaths when they succumb to the spill.

Yet orcas are also killer whales. Rather than glamorize or gloss over their role as formidable predators, Saulitis delves into the murky emotional territory she discovers through watching orcas hunt. Below, she describes an encounter with four orcas catapulting a porpoise in the air and eventually causing the creature's demise:

> I leaned across the dash, snapping photographs, my heart pounding, a sob stuck in my throat. Finish it off, I thought. Get it, I thought. "Oh my God, oh, my God, oh, my God," I said aloud to no one ... Here was nature, red in tooth. Here was suffering. Here was death. Here was the black-and-white, muscled, ruthless will to survive.

The author makes us privy to her efforts to reconcile predation and death—a reconciliation made all the more poignant given her own struggle with cancer. Consider this passage:

> Yet the idea of co-evolution—predator and prey influencing each other over millennia—spins what seems merciless, the absence of moral order, into something elegant, a dance of survival.

Perhaps within the chase itself, animals enact
what is already encoded deep in their cellular
structure. Because death is fate. And animals—
us included—are born knowing how to die.

With exceptional candor, Saulitis blurs the lines of scientific
inquiry and self-exploration such that her readers cannot
help but see orcas from her empathetic point of view, and
to be struck with the injustices that spilled forth from the
Exxon Valdez that ominous March night. Saulitis evokes the
ecological effects of the spill primarily by illuminating its
ramifications on her interior world, which were deeply etched
in her memory and captured in her research logs and journal.

Saulitis also grapples openly with the scientific paradigm
itself, alluding to the need to balance biological investigation
with other ways of knowing. As an ecologist committed to
doing exhaustive (and exhausting) field research with orcas,
she nonetheless recognizes that her role as the seer is one of
careful contemplation as well as observation. After using a
hydrophone to record orca calls, for example, Saulitis asks
herself what she's really learned as a result:

> It was as if an inverse relationship existed between
> data and knowing, as if the small pictures needed
> to accrue, the window into their lives first get
> more clouded, before the glass cleared and a big
> picture clarified.

Later in the book, Saulitis continues: "It takes decades for
the final alchemy to occur: observation into insight, data into
understanding, knowledge into wisdom. Eyes of innocence,
turning questions over to the mind, mind working the

questions until the grit rubs off and some truth emerges." Saulitis consistently incorporates humility and uncertainty into her writing in a way that, paradoxically, inspires confidence in her integrity as a scientist and a person. She dedicated her career to searching for deeper truths in the waters of Prince William Sound. Like Leopold, she found those truths through the eyes of a wild predator.

The Ninemile Wolves

In *The Ninemile Wolves*, his widely acclaimed book about wolves in Montana, Rick Bass conjures a unique blend of scene, exposition, and reflection to transcend biology and immerse his readers in the wonders of wild carnivores. Although Bass doesn't shy away from promoting his pro-wolf stance, his lyrical style both softens and strengthens his message such that only the steeliest of readers could part ways with *The Ninemile Wolves* without heightened respect for wolves—if not chagrin for our own species' cruelty on their behalf.

Wolves are travelers by nature and generally don't lend themselves well to intimate observation; most wolf researchers spend a lot of time chasing signals from radio collars and following tracks and other signs. Given this limitation, Bass's persuasiveness on behalf of wolves lies mainly in his ability to engage readers with his distinctive persona and that of his main character, wolf biologist Mike Jimenez. We quickly come to recognize these men for their commitment to wolves, and to empathize with the wolves from their unique and impassioned perspectives. While Bass presents himself as a philosophical thinker with scientific leanings, Jimenez is portrayed as a biologist who wrestles with the ethics of wolf management. The two personalities complement each other well, serving to both challenge and validate one another's sentiments on the scientific approach to understanding wolves.

Bass's persona is that of a gentle iconoclast. From the start, he makes it clear that—although he's scientifically informed—his opinions will not be constrained by the decorum of science: "I can say what I want to say. I gave up my science badge a long time ago." Thus, we come to know our narrator as a knowledgeable person who can be trusted to express himself, even if his opinions sometimes serve to test those of Jimenez and the other biologists with whom he associates. Bass emphasizes his identity as an independent thinker repeatedly throughout the book: "The wolves' nutritional demands are greater then, with extra hunting required to take care of the pups and, I propose (*which I can do, being a writer and not a biologist*) [emphasis added], it's possible that the rest of the pack gets plain restless during the denning period."

In the passage above, Bass invokes science to explain what might be going on when livestock depredation increases during the spring pupping season, but then speculates at a more anthropomorphic level. He further invites us into his worldview by revealing his inner conflict about wolf management and the difficulties faced by those working to move it forward. Bass's humble, self-deprecating voice tempers his unorthodox ideas to help make them more palatable to those who could otherwise shun them. Consider his ruminations on how wolves might find comfort in a train whistle:

> A train's faint moan reaches us from the next valley, and I wonder what the wolves think of that—if they ever call back to it. Is it outlandish to think maybe that's one of the things that drew them to this valley—that they were lonely, and

liked its sound? I'm thinking like a poet. I'm
thinking foolishly, stupidly.

Here, Bass appeases his more scientifically inclined audience
by deeming his own thinking outlandish, yet nonetheless
succeeds in encouraging us to think like a wolf. The
benefits of conceding one's idiosyncratic ideas in this way
are acknowledged in Phillip Lopate's *The Art of the Personal
Essay*: "The spectacle of baring the naked soul is meant to
awaken the sympathies of the reader, who is apt to forgive the
essayist's self-absorption in return for the warmth of his or her
candor ... Part of our trust in good personal essayists issues,
paradoxically, from their exposure of their own betrayals,
uncertainties, and self-mistrust."

Bass is a man unafraid to question his own beliefs.
Meanwhile, Jimenez's character—formally rooted in science
but as passionate as a proud father about the animals he
studies—brings additional credibility and balance to Bass's
musings about wolves. At one point, Bass conveys his
amazement about how wolves are somehow able to trail one
another over huge expanses of time and space. Jimenez clearly
shares his awe, and replies: "They just *follow* each other.
Nobody ever gave 'em that kind of credit." Together, Bass and
Jimenez embolden readers to reconsider their preconceived
notions concerning wolves.

In a sense, Jimenez is depicted as a lone wolf himself, out
there doing what needs to be done on behalf of the predators
who have breached his scientific boundaries. By revealing
Jimenez as a conflicted person in his own right, Bass stimulates
empathy for his role as a government scientist. Anecdotally,
I found Jimenez to be true-to-form with the character Bass
created in his book when I spoke with him at a wildlife

conference in Oregon. After listening to his presentation about wolf recovery in the Rocky Mountains, I solicited his opinion on the government-sanctioned killing of an entire family of wolves in northeastern Washington—wolves that were allegedly habituated to cattle. He earnestly replied that lethal control "definitely makes you sad" but comes with the territory of wolf recovery, thus echoing one of his quotes from *The Ninemile Wolves*: "The goal is to recover the population. The problem is that you do it through individuals—and when you deal with 'em on a continuous basis, it's real tough. You try not to get involved."

Fortunately, writers are less constrained. Like Bass and the other authors discussed in this paper, I consider it part of my mission to get emotionally involved with the predators I study and to relay this emotion to my readers. Alas, *The Ninemile Wolves* is especially pertinent to my current conundrum about wolves in Washington as I try to strike a healthy balance between my identities as a field biologist, an advocate, and an artist. As Bass contends: "It'll break your heart if you follow this story too closely, and for too long, with too much passion. It's never going to end. At least, I hope it doesn't ever end."

The Snow Leopard

The works of creative nonfiction discussed above are just a sampling of those presumably written in part to help ensure that the story of the planet's wild predators, and the animals inhabiting those stories, never end—at least not because of us. There are many other important books in this category (e.g., *The Snow Leopard* by Peter Matthiessen, *Of Wolves and Men* by Barry Lopez, *Jaguar* by Alan Rabinowitz, *Dominion of Bears* by Sherry Simpson, *The Wolverine Way* by Doug

Chadwick, *Grizzly Years* by Doug Peacock), and I assume the list will grow dramatically in the coming years given the plight of predators around the globe.

Although these books are as different in form and style as they are in subject matter, they are unified in their commitment to telling the truth about predators *and* telling it slant, to borrow from Emily Dickinson. Some authors rely heavily on observations while others focus their field glasses more inwardly. Peter Matthiessen never saw a single snow leopard during his two-month journey in the remote Himalayas of Nepal but nevertheless managed to bring this ghostly animal into public awareness by transporting his readers to the glacial shadows where snow leopards and blue sheep dance the ancient dance of predators and prey everywhere.

Matthiessen's brilliant book compelled me to ask myself: What does it really mean to *see* a snow leopard? As both symbols and keystones of wildness, can predators really be disentangled from the experience of place? Recently, during a behind-the-scenes tour at Seattle's Woodland Park Zoo, I was graced with the presence of a flesh-and-blood snow leopard—even touched his fur with my fingertip. Yet it occurred to me as I looked into those icy-moss eyes that Matthiessen encountered more snow-leopard-ness in the northern reaches of Nepal than I or a million other zoo-goers could imagine by gazing through the bars of a cage. I do hope and believe that watching animals in captivity can ignite the imagination and help generate long-term change. But only among those glacial shadows could the true essence of the snow leopard's wildness be absorbed through the human senses and translated to words on a page—an eternal gift that Matthiessen left us upon his death in 2014.

Concluding Thoughts

There's no getting around the fact that predators can be frightening, and that they're occasionally dangerous to humans. But each of the authors above presents us with the notion that there are other ways to see these powerful creatures, and that, if we can begin to strip away our biases and judgments, we can coexist with them in the future. As Turner proposes: "We might still, at this late moment, hold a predator—the ultimate Other—to our heart, might actually come to love its wild and utterly different life, might actually achieve a unity." If we don't, we are destined to suffer a great loss with profound ramifications. No more polar bears. No more tigers. No more grizzly bears. No more lions. *These* are the fears that keep me awake in my tent at night.

And then there is the importance of language itself. Although it doesn't benefit predators to rob them of their wildness by taming the terms used to describe them (to call a grizzly bear *cuddly*, for instance), Bekoff reminds us: "The words we use to refer to animals strongly influence how we view them and the actions we take to protect them." (Interestingly, the term *predator*, which means plunderer in Latin—*praedator*—has come to connote victimization and exploitation in our society.) We must choose our words carefully when writing about wildlife and use language that helps move people toward a more empathetic point of view. Turner writes: "Old ways of seeing do not change because of evidence; they change because a new language captures the imagination." He continues:

> Some people fear that extending a human vocabulary to wild animals erodes their Otherness. But what is not Other? Are we not all

from one perspective, Other to each and every being in the universe? And at the same time, and from another perspective, do we not all share an elemental wildness that burns forth in each life?

An excellent example of language as catalyst emerges from the work of biologist Gordon Haber, whose forty-three-year study of wolves in Alaska culminated in Marybeth Holleman's *Among Wolves* after Haber's death in 2009. Haber spent his long career fighting for wolf protection, and advocated the use of the word "family" to describe a social group of wolves because "pack" tends to have negative connotations:

> The use of the term "family" with regard to wolves is sometimes belittled in Alaska. However, any biologist who belittles the use of this term for wolves or other species reveals his or her ignorance of the scientific literature and knowledge about one of the most active areas in all of science—sociobiology—and may also be betraying his own underlying social or political agenda.

Which brings me back full-circle to Washington's Huckleberry wolves. A few days after one of the wolves was shot from the air, officials announced they had accidentally targeted the pack's alpha female. More to the point, they had lethally removed—*killed*—a mother with young pups on the ground. Ultimately, the rancher involved agreed to move his 1,800 sheep to another area for the remainder of the season. Conservationists cried too little too late. The fate of the remaining Huckleberry family is unknown.

The world is awash in gray. Sometimes men who kill wolves later become their champions, and occasionally, good people lose livestock or even their lives to wild predators. Injured tigers prowl villages because they are unable to hunt their natural prey; dispersing wolves travel hundreds of miles in search of mates. Yes, there are many, many stories to be told. Some of them even hold the power to rewild our hearts.

WORKS CITED

Bass, Rick. 1992. *The Ninemile Wolves*. New York: Ballantine Books.

Bekoff, Marc. 2014. *Rewilding our Hearts*. Novato: New World Library.

Eisenberg, Cristina. 2014. *The Carnivore Way: Coexisting with and Conserving North America's Predators*. Washington, D.C.: Island Press.

Haber, Gordon, and Marybeth Holleman. 2013. *Among Wolves*. Fairbanks: University of Alaska Press.

Leopold, Aldo. 1987. *A Sand County Almanac and Sketches Here and There*. Oxford: Oxford University Press.

Lopate, Phillip. 1995. *The Art of the Personal Essay*. New York: Anchor Books.

Matthiessen, Peter. 1987. *The Snow Leopard*. New York: Penguin Books.

Pancake, Ann. 2013. "Creative Responses to Worlds Unraveling: The Artist in the 21st Century." *The Georgia Review*, LXVII, Number 3: 409–410.

Quammen, David. 2003. *Monster of God*. New York: W. W. Norton & Company.

Saulitis, Eva. 2013. *Into Great Silence*. Boston: Beacon Press.

Turner, Jack. 1996. *The Abstract Wild*. Tucson: The University of Arizona Press.

Vaillant, John. 2010. *The Tiger*. New York: Alfred A. Knopf.

Rabies Bites: How Stephen King Made a Dog a Compelling Main Character

Hannah Sandoval

Two hundred pounds of muscle, foaming mouth, gnashing teeth, and burning amber eyes. Man's best friend turned savage beast. Cujo has instilled fear in readers since his creation in the early 1980s not because he's a massive dog who rips out people's throats. No, Cujo is a compelling, if terrifying, character because he started out as a quintessential good dog, and we witness his tragic transformation at the mercy of the rabies virus.

"Cujo likes kids." This is repeated multiple times in Cujo's first starring scene.

When the Trenton family in Stephen King's horror classic *Cujo* meet the slobbery Saint Bernard, no bat has yet sunk its rabies-infested teeth into the big dog's muzzle. Cujo is obedient. Cujo is sweet tempered. Cujo loves kids. The loveable bear of a dog allows four-year-old Tad Trenton to hug him, pat him, stick his hands in his mouth, throw him a ball, and even ride on his back. When little Tad falls, Cujo picks him up gently by the shirt collar and stands him upright.

When this story starts, Cujo is a protagonist—a gentle giant with a love of children. By the end, Cujo's brutal, rabies-fueled rampage leads to the death of the very child we saw him take such good care of in his very first scene. More than that, Cujo is a character we understand and sympathize with. Many times in literature, a dog is just a set piece: a funny, loyal companion to the main character who gives a few laughs. Many times in horror stories, an animal is used as a set piece whom the villain can kill off in order to earn himself the wrath of the reader. Not Cujo. Cujo is the star, the title character. His complexity makes him both terrifying and pitiable. How does King achieve this? How does he make this dog more than just a set piece?

The answer is twofold. First, King gives Cujo a clear character arc, or perhaps in this case, a character downward spiral. Second, King expertly gives us Cujo's perspective in a way that feels realistic, while allowing us to witness and feel firsthand the change that the rabies virus inflicts on Cujo's mind.

Though Cujo's first scene is sweet and creates in the reader an instant affinity for the dog, by itself, it would make Cujo nothing more than a cute little side note. Cujo's real story begins when he is bitten by the rabies-infected bat. This is what is classically known in fiction as the "inciting incident," the event that starts the main problem. Cujo's introduction serves to make us feel a connection to this dog before the real story gets started only two pages later. The character arc begins when Cujo is infected.

This scene plays out as a human character's scene would. King takes his time, describing how Cujo chases a rabbit into a small cave and gets himself stuck, open to attack by the bats. Most important, we get a glimpse into Cujo's thoughts. We see parts of the scene through Cujo's eyes. We know his emotions, his desires, and his fears.

The greatest example of King's expertise with this technique comes after Cujo has pulled himself out of the cave entrance, his muzzle bleeding from a bat bite.

> Dogs have a sense of self-consciousness that is far out of proportion to their intelligence, and Cujo was disgusted with himself. He didn't want to go home. If he went home, one of his trinity—THE MAN, THE WOMAN, or THE BOY—would see that he had done something to himself. It was possible that one of them might call him BADDOG. And at this particular moment he certainly considered himself to be a BADDOG.

Notice how King uses narration to portray Cujo's thoughts. He doesn't give us the direct thoughts from Cujo's head. Animals do not think in words because they do not speak. Giving your animal character actual thought quotes is unrealistic. Trying to simulate a dog's raw emotion through some sort of stream of consciousness would be too mumbled for the reader to really comprehend or engage. Some might try to give Cujo direct thoughts and put them in simplified language, as one would a child; this option risks making the animal more of a caricature or child's cartoon rather than a compelling character.

Instead, King uses narration to give the reader a *sense* of Cujo's thoughts without actually plopping the reader into his head. He does this subtly, by capitalizing the names Cujo has given his masters and by calling them "his trinity." This gives us a sense of Cujo's loyalty, admiration, and even awe for the humans in his life. Capitalizing the chastisement of "bad dog" and cramming the words together shows us that Cujo doesn't understand this term as words per se, only as a terrible ideal that he wishes to avoid. BADDOG is one of his greatest fears.

King's line about a dog's self-consciousness will ring true to any dog owner who has met with the slinking body, tucked tail, and upturned pleading eyes of a dog who knows he or she has done wrong. This line, though not a thought of Cujo's, gives weight and realism to the expression of Cujo's feelings because it connects with the reader's own experience.

After the inciting incident, we lose touch with Cujo for a little while and catch up with the other main characters. However, when we return to him, Cujo's character arc is well under way. He faces his first pinch point (a conflict that applies pressure to the character) in the shape of Gary Pervier. Gary is a war vet with a nasty temper who doesn't get along with most folks, but the old man adores Cujo, and Cujo is fond of him. The dog goes to visit Gary every day, just to lie around and give him company. Once again, Cujo's lovable personality is confirmed by Gary's opinion that he is "one of your old-fashioned, dyed-in-the-wool good dogs." But Cujo's villain, rabies, has started to affect him. When Gary gives him a treat, Cujo just mouths it until Gary urges him to eat. When Gary attempts to pet Cujo, Cujo growls. Our chests tighten. Here, the reader worries for Cujo. The reader likes this dog and doesn't want to see this change. *Fight it, Cujo*, the reader thinks. And fight he does. "Cujo wagged his tail a little bit and came over to Gary to be patted, as if ashamed of his momentary lapse." The reader breathes a sigh of relief. Sweet Cujo has won his first battle against the rabies addling his brain. But by now there's a question nagging the reader, one that can't be ignored: Just how long can Cujo fight?

Cujo's second pinch point (in which hope seems lost for the character) is when the disease urges him to turn on Brett Camber—THE BOY. We know that Cujo loves Brett more than anyone else in the world, but when Brett calls his dog to tell him goodbye before going on a trip, Cujo materializes out of the fog a matted, snarling, foaming beast.

> Cujo looked at THE BOY, not recognizing him any more, not his looks, not the shadings of his clothes ... not his scent. What he saw was a monster on two legs. Cujo was sick, and all things appeared monstrous to him now. His head clanged dully with murder. He wanted to bite and rip and tear.

This use of perspective is jarring (and extremely powerful) because the reader has taken part in Cujo's feelings and thoughts before, and this does not sound like the character the reader knows. This makes the change in Cujo all the more terrible. Again, the reader roots for him, more than ever. The reader knows that the real, pre-rabies Cujo would hate himself if he ever hurt Brett. *Fight it, Cujo, you can do it.*

In this moment, Cujo becomes a hero. Brett says Cujo's name, and he recognizes his master. Still, the disease is urging him to attack. The reader watches with baited breath as Cujo fights.

Once he had loved THE BOY and would have died for him, had that been called for. There was enough of that feeling left to hold the image of murder at bay until it grew as murky as the fog around them ... The last of the dog that had been before the bat scratched its nose turned away, and the sick and dangerous dog, subverted for the last time, was forced to turn with it.

This point raises a new question: Is Cujo really the villain? In a literal sense, yes. It is Cujo the physical dog who goes on to kill people. However, Cujo is a sympathetic antagonist (arguably the most powerful kind in literature) because the ultimate villain, rabies, has made him unrecognizable.

We cheer Cujo's victory here, but we also mourn. If this was a hero character arc, Cujo would move on to a happy resolution after overcoming his second pinch point. However, Cujo's arc is a tragedy, so though he wins the second pinch point's battle, he loses the war. The Cujo we have come to care for has had his shining moment of heroism, fighting with all that is left in him, but it is also the start of the downward slope of his character arc.

King's third-person omniscient narration allows us to understand Cujo's way of thinking here—the havoc the disease is wreaking on his brain and his strong feelings for Brett—and lets us know that this will be the last time the protagonist side of Cujo wins out.

This becomes all too obvious when Cujo kills Gary Pervier, the war vet he had befriended. Once again, we get a glimpse into Cujo's state of mind just as he approaches Gary, fangs bared. "[Cujo] suddenly understood THE MAN had made him sick." The capitalization of THE MAN has a different meaning here. Cujo doesn't know who Gary is. He is just a being, a frightening villain whom Cujo believes is responsible for his constant pain. There is a moment, after he first bites Gary, when Cujo almost backs down, but his arc has taken a downward tilt. "He hurt, he hurt so miserably, and the world was such a crazyquilt [*sic*] of sense and impression—" This could also be seen as the first pinch point to the second Cujo, the rabies-addled Cujo. He faces his first conflict and, to his mind, comes out on top.

Let's run with the idea that our sweet, lovable Cujo died a hero in his final climactic battle where he chose not to attack Brett. Now, the reader witnesses the story of Rabies Cujo as he forms his own arc. Rabies Cujo's second pinch point comes when Joe Camber, Cujo's owner, goes looking for Gary. He comes upon Gary's dead body and the ferocious Rabies Cujo himself. If there was any doubt that Cujo had lost himself completely to the disease, it is squashed when he kills Joe Camber, unable to turn away as he did with Brett. In fact, Cujo's perspective is missing from this scene altogether, further distancing the reader from him and signaling that the real Cujo is no more.

We do not see the Saint Bernard's perspective for a very long time, in fact. We do not get a sense for what sends him into a rage when Tad and Donna Trenton (the mother and son Cujo met in his opening scene) bring their car to the Camber home for repair. We do not know how he feels when Donna's car stalls as she tries to drive away and gets stuck in the relentless summer sun in the Camber yard. We do not know, at least not firsthand, why he slams his body into the car over and over again, beating himself bloody in his attempt to dispatch the Trentons.

When we do finally get a glimpse into Rabies Cujo's

head, it is a very different place. Rabies Cujo is plotting, as much as a dog can plot. He is lying in wait under the front of the Trentons' car, waiting for Donna to come out. King uses clever narration to put this change into perspective.

> As the sickness had tightened down on [Cujo], sinking into his nervous system like a ravenous grassfire, all dove-gray smoke and low rose-colored flame, as it continued to go about its work of destroying his established patterns of thought and behavior, it had somehow deepened his cunning.

Rabies Cujo is a terror. Though rage fuels him, he is not yet so far gone that he cannot be calculating as well. He is a predator, and he has locked in on his prey. "He would wait until he could get at them. If necessary he would wait until the world ended."

Still, King is careful to remind the reader that even Rabies Cujo is to be pitied. We see him try to drink, "but the actual sight of the water had driven him into a frenzy." Rabies Cujo longs for water, but he cannot drink. His brain revolts each time he tries, and he retreats, "whining and trembling." In the middle of this tense moment, where everything else about Cujo's new perspective should tell us to hate him, King inserts this pitiable moment, making even Rabies Cujo a complex and sympathetic villain.

At this point, Rabies Cujo has reached the beginning of his climax. When Donna Trenton tries to run for the Cambers' house and the phone within, Cujo attacks. She manages to fight him off, but the policeman who comes looking for the Trentons is not so lucky. Again, Rabies Cujo's motivations and feelings are expertly shown through King's narration when Cujo looks at the cop.

> THE MAN had caused the pain in his joints and the high, rotten singing in his head; it was THE MAN'S fault that the drift of old leaves here beneath the porch now smelled putrescent; it was THE MAN'S fault that he could not look at water without whining and shrinking away and wanting to kill it in spite of his great thirst.

Rabies Cujo's final battle marks the end of Cujo's tragedy. Donna Trenton has had enough. Her little boy is dying of heat exposure. Bloody and bruised, like her foe, she leaves the safety of the car, grabs Brett Camber's baseball bat from the yard, and faces off with the already dying Saint Bernard. Even in his final moment of savagery, we are reminded of the real Cujo and the lunacy that is driving his final act before Donna brings his life to an end. "For the last time the dying ruin that had been Brett Camber's good dog Cujo leaped at THE WOMAN that had caused all his misery."

When Cujo is gone, the reader does feel a sense of relief for Donna and Tad, but the reader can't help but be saddened at Cujo's demise. After all, "He was one of your bona fide good dogs."

To create such a conflict of feelings in this ending, King had to make Cujo more than just a scary set piece—a distant terror or an unnamed shadow that leaps from the dark. He let the reader get to know Cujo, understand him, even as he slipped into madness. He did so by using subtle, third-person omniscient narrative techniques to give the reader a sense of Cujo's mind without plunging unrealistically into the actual brain of a dog. He gave Cujo a fully developed character arc, just like all the other main human characters in the story. One could even argue he went the extra mile and gave him two.

The next time you sit down to write a story that features an animal, think about how you can make that animal undergo a change. Even if the animal is not in as prominent a role as Cujo, secondary characters can have arcs, too, even if they're small ones. If you want to give your readers a sense of that animal's personality and motivations, do so through both action and through subtle narration, as demonstrated here through King's work. If you want your readers to really care about the animal in your story, you need to devote just as much time and attention to that animal as any of your human characters.

Those who know of *Cujo* only through word of mouth or the film adaptation might think *Cujo* demonstrates animal cruelty or perpetuates fear of dogs, but readers of the book know differently. In *Cujo,* King shows his readers just how scary the idea of fate can be—small, seemingly irrelevant factors coming together to form a nightmarish scenario in which good people (and dogs) clash violently—and whether intentionally or not, he makes a powerful argument for the importance of rabies vaccinations.

Works Cited

King, Stephen. 1981. *Cujo*. New York: Viking.

Real Advocacy within Fantasy Worlds

Beth Lyons

Clarity came about two-thirds of the way through writing my first novel: a vital element was missing. One of my main characters, a magical healer named Indira, hadn't eaten anything. Ever. Almost 70,000 words, and the poor woman hadn't even nibbled on a crust of bread.

I'd been vegan almost a year when I started writing that story, and without realizing it, I'd avoided the question of adding veganism to it by eliminating food from the narrative. The story is classic fantasy—the stuff I love to read—filled with magic and swords and epic battles. I knew that my magic users would wear robes, and my warriors would wear leath—wait, leather? No. Not in my story. Nixing leather armor was easy, but I couldn't avoid food.

In modern fantasy, food is more than just calories, more than just a prop. Food illustrates wealth, position, power. Hunting food, preparing it, eating it—these actions move the narrative along, functioning as world-building units of fiction. Where someone hunts, what they eat, how it's cooked … these are authorial choices that will impact how a reader views the story, even if they're vegan. Especially if they're vegan.

But what does it mean to be a vegan writer? Can, for example, the hero of your fantasy novel hunt animals for food? Or is that reserved solely for the villain? Can you portray a feast that features meat as the main dish? Do vegan writers have a duty to present vegan options in their stories, or can they simply tell their stories and leave real-world politics alone?

Fiction gives us a channel to introduce unfamiliar and even controversial subjects to readers, and genre fiction in particular lends itself to this endeavor. Characters with strange names and strange customs are interesting, not threatening. For readers, it need not impact their real lives if a fictional religion preaches veganism or if a novel's character is repulsed by goat's-milk cheese. They come for the story; they come to be transported to a new world.

On one level, being a vegan writer is no different than being a vegan—our lives are filled with abundance. Detractors say, "It's such a strict diet!" We reply, "It's not a diet, and let's talk about the abundant food choices vegans have!" Which brings us right back to fictional food, doesn't it? Even fictional characters have to eat. My healer, running across the landscape of Sarana, needed sustenance. I had to view it not as a problem but as an opportunity to expand both my fictional world and, possibly, my readers' mindsets.

One of the best compliments I've gotten about my novel *The Soul Thief* isn't even a compliment: It's the fact that no one has complained about the vegan and animal-rights themes.

To solve the problem of Indira's hunger, I had to think about the world I'd created. Indira received her magical training through a religious order, and diet is often a religious tenet. So far, so good. I could make a whole group of people vegan, and no one would pause.

Healers by their nature are going to be compassionate people anyway, so even though some people might follow some parts of a religion but not others, my healer would be a staunch, compassionate advocate for animals. Ah, but what does that mean, and how does that actually look within the confines of a novel? Who wants to read pages of preachy dialogue about animal rights?

Enter the foil. My healer, Indira, would explain her world view to another character (and therefore to the reader). If one character is a vegan healer, the other one could be a meat-eating thief. Opposites attract, and more important, opposites allow for exposition. In the world of Sarana, the ruling class mostly adheres to a vegan diet, and only the poor and outcast eat animals. My two main characters, with their opposing world views and life experiences, have to find a way to work together. Opposition creates tension, which is the fuel of narrative. In other words, it's good writing and good advocacy because the characters are forced to work through their cultural differences.

Idiomatic expressions are one way for writers to bolster the cultures that support their fantasy worlds. A well-placed adage can do the work of a page of description or exposition. Classic fantasy settings tend to downplay technology—a fantasy novel's world will likely be filled with fields, plows, and beasts of burden; the hero will be a simple farm boy or girl from a village ruled by a lord who in turn answers to a king or queen. The humans make the rules and enforce them, but their well-being rests on the ox's shoulders. Food, clothing, tools, and weapons all come from animals.

Many of our Western sayings originated from an agrarian mindset—no counting chickens until they hatch, no crying over spilled milk, no closing the barn door after the horse has run free—making it all too easy to carry those sayings over into our classic fantasy settings without alteration. That authorial choice (often not even a conscious one) can foster the mindset that animals are here for our use.

So what's a vegan writer to do? Make up her own idioms, of course! Instead of cautioning against counting chickens before they hatch, a character can say, "No one ever baked a pie with apple blossoms." Or "Flowers don't fill the apple barrel." A mother could comfort an upset child by saying, "Tears won't mend a broken bowl." When neighbors want to gossip about another's folly, they could say, "No use locking the shed now that the axe is gone." Making a worn adage into something new catches readers' imaginations and helps hold them in the fictive dream.

Now we have a setting, characters, some good reasons to be vegan in this fictional world, and a way to talk about it within the structure of a fantasy setting. What about the animals, though? Classic fantasy tropes tend to eschew machines. Need to travel any distance? Use a horse. Are you a farmer? Yoke up your oxen to plow that field. Staying at an inn? No doubt you'll find a dead animal roasting over a fire. Readers expect these set pieces. These and a hundred other small things like leather boots, waterskins, fur-lined cloaks, and feather beds, make up the "reality" of a fantasy novel. Animals (and their parts) are often reduced to elaborate props for an author to use to paint the canvas.

I made mistakes with that first novel. Eating animals was

clearly wrong, but riding horses? Not so much. I struck the middle-ish path of having the religious order only use horses that they'd raised themselves. Freakish to non-vegan readers, no doubt, but questionable (at the very least) to readers who care about animal rights.

I found another mistake late in the editing process. I realized that I had unthinkingly used the term *waterskin* to describe the device to hold water. No way that would be vegan. A few find-and-replace commands later, *waterskin* was gone, replaced by the pedestrian *canteen*. Maybe not quite so fantastical but certainly more animal-friendly.

Now, several years and a few books later, it's difficult for me to write scenes in which any character, even a non-vegan one, would ride a horse, yoke an ox, roast a dead animal. My sensibilities have changed and so, too, has my writing. But is it my duty to write this way?

Stories are powerful. The lessons nestled inside them are powerful, too. When people read my stories, they enter my reality. In order for them to stay, my world needs to be consistent and logical within itself. If I've done my job, if the narrative is consistent and persistent, readers can suspend their disbelief for the duration of the novel, absorbing the logic and culture of my vegan world.

That might not sound like much of a victory—someone reading a 300-page book that features vegan characters. Could a fantasy novel really inspire readers to go vegan? Well, it might at least make them think about farm animals in a new way, or it might tip the scale and convince someone to try being vegan for a month, but the reality probably falls somewhere in the middle.

So is it my duty to tell vegan stories? Perhaps *duty* is too strong a word; call it a compulsion. I am compelled to write stories in which animals are not harmed, in which people don't eat them or use them, and I'm not alone. Independent presses, publishers, and outlets like Amazon and Smashwords allow vegan authors like me the chance to share our stories.

Stories are real-world magic with the power to change hearts, and every day, the body of stories that consider more than humans and their needs grows. Readers are looking for vegan worlds to explore, and authors who might otherwise compartmentalize their activism from their writing have opportunities to be a voice for animals while giving voice to their creative vision.

Writing Animals Where You Are

Hunter Liguore

So you want to write about animals?

Okay.

If you had to choose between the snow leopard, the bald eagle, and a mouse, which would you pick?

I'm guessing you won't choose the mouse. (And if you did, awesome!)

But here's why.

More often, when given a choice, writers pick the animals that are rare and uncommon. There is a general sense that common animals—the mouse, the cat, the cardinal—are too familiar to the reader. But that's not necessarily true. So rather than write what is available, writers go to great lengths to search out greater sights, missing many opportunities to share the animal world right where they live—every single day.

Getting Started

Today, let's try a new path, one that will allow you to rediscover the animal world living right where you are. No need to hit the trails, or plan a fancy vacation—there are plenty of animals right near you who are in need of a writer.

Whether you live in a busy city, a college dorm, an apartment, or are riding the bus, animals are there to meet you.

When we choose to recognize the animal world most available to us, we open up so many opportunities to reconnect, essentially eliminating the false boundaries between us and them.

Our relationships with animals aren't separate.

Though it may seem as though animals live outside and we live inside, we're engaging in a reciprocal relationship, one constantly in flow and in harmony—if we're willing to shift our perception and recognize it.

When we rediscover the numerous animals all around us—at all times—we can not only write about them, we can deepen our understanding of animals and strengthen our relationships, which we ultimately carry forward, to others, through our writing.

Step One—The List

Items you'll need: a nature journal or cellphone to record your findings.

Assignment: Spend an hour, a day, or a week rediscovering the animals you encounter on a daily basis. Look and acknowledge even the smallest critter. Write a short reflection about what you see.

Questions to consider: Where are animals meeting you? What do you see when you look out the window?

The animal you write about might be inside the head of lettuce you got from the grocery store. Or perhaps it's a house spider or ant that came out of hiding. Perhaps it's the neighbor's cat, or the pigeons in the park you see along the bus route.

Give yourself permission to recognize what's been there all along. Notice the birds in the sky, or sitting on streetlights, on the way to and from your destinations. Be observant—on some mornings, I can count twenty red-tailed hawks during an hour-long drive, while my colleagues traveling the same road see none.

What's important is to begin to acknowledge that there is life creeping and crawling at every level: the tiniest ants and insects; foxes, squirrels, skunks, and deer; ducks in the park; the seagulls hanging out at the fast-food joints.

Animals are everywhere.

Write down the animals you see. Describe them in as much detail as you can. For instance: where you encountered the animals; what they looked like; their coloring or size; what they were doing; what the environment looked like. It's not about seeing the most animals but your ability to be aware of your surroundings and what is available to you.

Example: *Stink beetle. Discovered in an upstairs bedroom, crawling up the window. It has four legs (I think, maybe six) and two antennae. It's all green. Shaped like a shield. Easy to put in a cup to bring outside. Once outside, it blended in with the grass. Watched it walking. Curious creature. Never seen one before. Had to look up what it was.*

Once you have the information, you might want to incorporate a memory the animal brings up for you. In the example above, it was a first encounter, so that could easily be expanded on by asking: What was it like to encounter a new species? If the encounter was with an animal you've seen before, like a ladybug, you might also write down the memory it brought up for you.

Example: *The ladybug landed on the windowsill, trying to get out. I watched it for so long, I could actually see where its real eyes were, against the fake ones meant to deter prey. It took me back to a time in my childhood when my sister and I were walking among the backyard flowers, which were covered in ladybugs—it was magical, like we'd encountered fairies.*

Continue to record the animals that show up for you each day. Be mindful not to give more importance to one type of animal over the other—all are equal. When you feel ready, after you've gotten familiar with the animals in your everyday world, move on to step two.

Step Two—Your Rediscovery Assignment

Items you'll need: a camera and a computer or nature journal.

Assignment: You're going to create a photo journey by taking three to five pictures of the animals you encounter in your daily life. Just as in the above exercise, the animals you encounter might be the ones you meet on the way to work or school, or at the supermarket. They may be those you see when you're out for a walk or in the comfort of your own home or garden, or even on vacation. Wherever you are, you can find animals—and all animals have something to share.

Note: You might take several pictures of the same animal, or several of one species, or multiple photos of all the different animals you meet. It is up to you to decide how you will interpret this.

Next, write a 250- to 450-word micro-essay for each picture, reflecting on the story behind the animals you captured with your camera. What stories do they have to tell? What feelings do they bring out in you—joy, fear, peace, contentment, spiritual connection, reciprocity, etc.? What do they have to teach you, and how do they inspire you? How do these animals impact your life? What wisdom might they share? Consider how their lives reflect back on yours (e.g., the skunk that everyone runs from can easily turn into an essay about social anxiety).

Each micro-essay should attempt to capture your ideas with the most precise words. You might format your photos to run side-by-side with the text.

Conclusion

When writers are willing to meet animals where they live, the hierarchy of certain animals being more important can fall away. What's more, writers can start working *right now*, without the impediment of waiting until a "better animal" comes along.

Last, and most important, we become solid witnesses to our world and can give voices to the animals we—and our readers—encounter more frequently. If I write about the mice in my attic, I might connect with someone who also has mice in the attic, or if I write about the groundhog that comes each season, I might share something and connect with someone who also sees groundhogs. Not everyone sees lions, tigers, and bears every day. Together, though, we can work to give voice to the diversity of the animal kingdom.

So go and write the animals you see—wherever you see them. The animals will thank you. You'll no doubt start to realize how much more we are all connected, sharing this Earth.

Part III:
Anthropomorphism and Literature

Other Nations

Marybeth Holleman

At some point during the forty-three years biologist Gordon Haber spent studying Alaska's wild wolves, he stopped using the word "pack" and began using the words "family group." He knew what his field observations had taught him about wolves, and he knew the power of language.

Haber watched dozens of families of wild wolves year-round in all kinds of conditions; he witnessed successive generations of the same wolf family groups as they developed distinctive methods of hunting, rearing pups, and communicating. What he concluded was that wolves are not at all what the word "pack" connotes: They aren't a "snarling aggregation of fighting beasts, each bent on fending only for itself," but rather a highly evolved, socially cohesive, cooperative community.

As writers, we know the power of language to reach people on a deeper level. Art bypasses the analytical mind and aims straight for memory and imagination. New research corroborates this: Reading (especially fiction) makes people more empathetic, more able to enter into the world of another, an Other. Story has power.

We wield this power when we write about/for/with animals—especially now, when their fate is so clearly and completely in our hands. That's why, thirty years ago, I turned from my work in environmental policy to creative writing. I realized that in story lies animals' salvation, and ours. But ever since, I've struggled with *how:* how to write about nonhuman lives as not just metaphor or setting for a human-centric story, but as central characters, critical to the story's unfolding.

I'm going to blame it all on Descartes. I blame the sixteenth-century philosopher for the difficulties we face in writing about nonhuman lives, writing about what David Abrams calls the more-than-human world: the thrumming, roaring, fully alive world of which we are just one species, just one kind of animal.

To Descartes, all living beings *except* humans were nothing more than automata, machines with fur and feather and fin. While science has proven this a simplification, it remains at the core of how nonhuman lives are treated. Thanks to Descartes, wildlife is "managed" according to the assumed objectivity of such measures as population statistics. And we writers are saddled with a conundrum when we try to write anything more than what science tells us to be true, lest we are accused of anthropomorphizing: of comparing them to us.

Well, of course they are not us. They aren't even each other. A robin is not a leopard is not a shark is not a human. They are, wrote Henry Beston, "other nations" who, with all their differences, their "extensions of the senses that we have lost or never attained … shall not be measured by man."

I carry Beston's words with me, a talisman against Cartesian simplification, as I continue my quest—how to write about other animals in a way that is of them, for them, with them. How to give voice, to allow them agency on the page, to peel back the layers we've applied so that they can emerge as fully themselves as possible. How to write about the world beyond the human realm in language that fully engages the reader and yet remains utterly truthful to the otherness of these other nations.

I've wandered these wilds repeatedly, from my first essay about trumpeter swans, in which I question the limits of scientific knowledge; to my memoir, *The Heart of the Sound*, an exploration of my evolving relationship to the wild inhabitants of Prince William Sound, a wilderness degraded by an oil spill; to my latest book, *Among Wolves*, as I share a wolf biologist's relationship with and insights into wild wolves.

I won't lie: I'm still learning. All I have to offer is what I've picked up along the way, like shells on a beach, as waves keep washing away and leaving more. I pile them up like cairns, so that each time I begin, again, to write about the more-than-human world, they lead the way.

Stand in the Middle

The most visible cairn is this: Writing about the nonhuman world is a practice in standing in the middle. Straddling sentimentality and detached hard-nosed Cartesian rigor without sliding lazily into anthropomorphism or leaning too far into anthropocentrism. Straddling the fact of degradation and loss, and the fact of the life and beauty that remains. Straddling the apparent otherness of nonhuman life, and the apparent similarities between us all, resonances of the more-than-human world. I aim to hold two seemingly opposing forces on the page at the same time.

Root in Unmediated Experience

It starts with direct, unmediated experience. Authentic writing about any Other—whether another culture or another species—must. This is what drew me to write about, and with, the late Gordon Haber: The thousands of hours he spent in the presence of wild wolves sets his work apart, makes it more authentic and aligned. What makes writing about wild animals authentic and aligned is the same: It is rooted in direct, unmediated experience. Unmediated experience is not filtered by other people, other ideas, screens, windows, stories, myths, any of the myriad layers that come between us and the Other; it is *felt* experience that engages all our senses.

In direct experience lies truth. But it takes time. Cezanne painted more than sixty versions of Mont Sainte-Victoire, continually trying to reveal one mountain. I wrote about the nonhuman lives of Prince William Sound after fifteen years of camping, kayaking, boating, hiking, beach cleaning, wildlife watching, and just being there, through the still sunny days and the driving snow and rain.

With time, moments arise, often when least expected. One late August day, I crouched in our inflatable as we crossed Port Wells in sideways rain and five-foot seas, wanting only to be home. Just off the bow, a sea lion popped up from the waves with a pink salmon in his mouth. He looked right at me, tossed the fish skyward, caught it in midair, gave me another hard look, then arced back underwater.

These are mostly the briefest of moments, for as I wrote in *The Heart of the Sound*, "It's lonely being human. When I see wild animals, I wish they wouldn't run or fly or swim off at my appearance; I wish they wouldn't be so frightened. I wish they enjoyed my presence the way I enjoy theirs."

As a writer, as a human on this planet, I am certain that

all living, real living, lies in these brief moments when the veil drops. Virginia Woolf called these "moments of being" that exist "behind the cotton wool of daily life," the very moments that we writers are beholden to recognize and reveal. Mary Austin had another term: "flashes of mutual awareness." Hers adds another dimension, moments when both the human and the Other—whether squirrel, arctic tern, or bear—are aware of each other. It's also been called Profound Interspecies Encounters, or PIE. Think Annie Dillard's weasel: I am aware of you at the same moment that you are aware of me, and for that moment, as long as it takes a shooting star to flame out, I can sense what it is like to be you. These are the gems, the small trailside treasures, feathers and stones and wisps of moose fur clinging to willow, that we writers carry to the page.

Be Clear, Curious, and Open-Minded

Experiencing these flashes of mutual awareness requires clarity of vision, curiosity, and open-mindedness about the Other that isn't conditioned by old stories, advertising, culture's mindless clichés, or reruns playing in the head—whether it's *Little Red Riding Hood*, Animal Planet's *Killer Cats*, or *The Wolf of Wall Street*. This can be tricky. As Sherry Simpson tells us in *Dominion of Bears*, what we think we know about bears comes mostly from story, not from direct experience. So what do we really know about a bear, the real actual being? We view bear through a glass darkly, clouded by layers of myth and assumptions.

To write about, and relate to, the shorebirds called oystercatchers, I had to shed what science told me about them; I had to crouch down on the beach and watch the waves, reach out a hand and flip over one pebble, then another; I had to softly hum, a gentle, consistent sound, before I could experience, ever so briefly, "a mutual awareness without fear": oystercatchers not flying off but coming toward me, looking right at me.

This isn't hard; it's something we know in our everyday lives. Say you're a backyard birdwatcher. You know that the more time you watch, say, robins, the more you can deduce from their behavior. You learn what the alarm call sounds like. You watch robins' body language when they make the alarm call or tap the ground for worms. You can write robin.

Anthropomorphism just threw its long shadow across the page, didn't it? When I shifted from journalism to creative writing, one of my first essays arose from tagging along with biologists researching trumpeter swans on Alaska's Copper River Delta. I sat with them watching swans from blinds; I flew over the delta, helping them count the pairs of cream-colored ovals surrounded by water, ice, and emerging green; I interviewed them and read their reports. I was curious about swans but not just about what science tells us about swans: I was curious about what life is like for a swan. And yet I was schooled well in the perils of anthropomorphism and feared I wouldn't be taken seriously as a writer if I fell into that pothole.

Don't Fear Anthropomorphism

The more time I've spent with swans, and bears, and oystercatchers, the more I've come to view anthropomorphism as I view the rules of grammar. I advise creative writing students to learn the rules of grammar before they break them. They must learn what a sentence is before they can successfully use a sentence fragment. It must be intentional, not a sloppy first draft or an outright error. It's the same with anthropomorphism: Know what it is, be aware of it, then write what direct experience shows to be true.

At a time when a mechanistic view of the natural world was replacing Aristotle's concepts, Descartes concluded that all nonhuman behavior can be explained in purely mechanistic terms, and, therefore, animals lack consciousness. As I wrote in *The Heart of the Sound*, "According to Descartes and his fellow philosophers of this Age of Reason, everything in the universe behaved according to a few simple mathematical laws—an oystercatcher was no more than a box of discernable parts that, when put together in a certain way, would perform like an oystercatcher. But I want more than a one-dimensional puzzle, a one-way river of information, more than this process of breaking down the lives of swans and oystercatchers into manageable pieces. Such breaking down into pieces, a Zen Buddhist master once said, actually separates worlds rather than bringing them together."

Researching *Among Wolves*, diving deep into the lifetime of work of one wolf biologist, I began to see how scientists' and writers' disdain for anthropomorphism can make them so removed that they view Other as not only nonhuman but *non-life*—reverting to a Cartesian simplification that denies reality. Wildlife is "managed" almost entirely by population, yet for many species, such as wolves, a measure of their overall health is not at all about numbers but about social structure, about family. Haber didn't anthropomorphize, and he had little patience for those who did. Instead, he let his decades of on-the-ground research lead him to conclusions—some that many in the wolf biology world are just now accepting, in large part because it's not convenient; it's much easier to manage by the numbers.

Scientists try to be objective toward the animals they study. Writers try to avoid romanticizing and sentimentality.

But it's not humanly possible to be entirely objective, for we are not automata, either. Instead, we risk falling into the trap of *anthropocentrizing*, of regarding humans as above and beyond the rest of the living world. I'll venture that our biggest fear in writing about the more-than-human world should be anthropocentrism, not anthropomorphism. As poet Gretchen Primack said, "What we're doing now is the absolute opposite of anthropomorphism. What if we erred on the side of respecting the other species too much? What would that look like?"

It's about standing in the middle: neither romanticizing nor mechanizing the Other but grounding it in actual unmediated experience. We can look for that middle ground, where animals are neither human nor robots—the middle ground where they truly live. The human brain has a strong tendency to look for connections and similarities to make sense of the new. That's why simile and metaphor work so well: The brain wants footing in new territory. So we can't help but make associations. But if we clear the cultural clutter, we might find connections that ring true.

One more thing about the perils of anthropomorphism-phobia. Remember Vivian Gornick's line about nature writing? "As a rule, I don't read nature writing, because I hardly ever get it. The metaphor always feels strained and the sensibility foreign—that hushed, saintly quiet in the narrating voice … " I have come to believe that it's our fear of anthropomorphizing that gives us this detached, hushed voice—a hush that can make the writing fall flat. Our job as writers is to interpret and find meaning, to move beyond the sum of the parts.

Include Scientific Knowledge

I love what science has to tell me about wildlife and wild places. It enriches my experience and expands my appreciation for the more-than-human world. After seeing a collared pika in a scree slope, I learned about their hay-making behavior, and my admiration for these tiny, nonhibernating mammals grew.

What I concluded in my essay on trumpeter swans was that science doesn't betray the mystery; it deepens it. That is, science provides information, but the information leads to more questions—which then strengthens the mystery. The lives of swans are immensely more complex than we can ever know, and as much as I wonder what it would be like to be one, I'm glad for the mystery. The key is remembering that our knowledge is limited: All too often, decisions about wild lives are made as if we know everything about them.

The poet Pattiann Rogers reminds us that the world responds to the questions we ask. Scientists ask certain kinds of questions and so get certain kinds of answers. We writers can ask different questions, can approach our felt experience from other angles. As we delve into scientific knowledge, we do well to remember the questions *we* might ask.

Science is only one kind of knowledge, as recent focus on Traditional Ecological Knowledge reminds us, but it is a necessary cairn. Too often I'll be reading an otherwise excellent poetry collection or short story and come to some off-handed reference to "the lone wolf" or "the wolf at the door." I am stopped, stunned, and disheartened by such careless and incorrect clichés. Haber pointed out that lone wolves die—"a wolf isn't a single animal"—for they depend on community to survive. Scientific accuracy is bedrock to the authority of our writing. Rooted in scientific fact and direct experience, we can loosen the stranglehold of anthropomorphism.

Remember the Human Filter

The cast of anthropomorphism is both what we need to shed and a reminder of our responsibility—that the stories we tell are as close to the truth as humanly possible. For let's be clear: We are human. We will always view the Other through the lens of being human. We are animals, and as such, share common experiences with our brethren in other nations—which we do well to remember. Still, regardless of how much I want to know what it's like to be an oystercatcher or a bear, I still can't fly or walk on four legs. Awareness of that filter is critical to seeing, and writing, clearly.

As Beston reminds us, "They are not brethren, they are not underlings; they are other nations, caught with ourselves in the net of life and time, fellow prisoners of the splendor and travail of the earth." It isn't possible to fully understand them, just as it's never possible to fully understand another human being. But that's what makes it all—the experience, the struggle, the writing—so wonderful.

Get Comfortable with Both/And

It is in complexity and apparent contradiction that truth lies. When I taught a course on the literature of mothering, I came across articles noting that a mother must engage *both/and* thinking, rather than the *either/or* thinking to which we humans are so accustomed. That is, rather than thinking there is only one right way to, say, get her baby to sleep through the night, or one right path for her middle-school son, a mother sees multiple options. And these options shift with every moment. She must hold apparent contradictions in her hands, and mind, at once. This isn't easy, given our cultural predilections.

Yet this is the way the world usually works—especially the

152

more-than-human world. Rarely is it one-size-fits-all. I have come upon cow moose with calves in early summer dozens of times, so now I know, from their body language, how much room I should give them, how much I should rein in my dogs as we pass. But I am also aware, and have experienced several times, that my knowledge is limited: At any moment, the cow might run straight away from me, or straight at me.

This both/and view is a vital cairn in allowing these nonhuman lives their own agency, in allowing their Otherness to remain intact. It's not just according basic worth to other species; it's describing, revealing, acknowledging it. It's remembering that we, too, are animals. They are us and not-us. This requires a sharp awareness of our own perceptions and our use of language.

Give Voice

In *The Heart of the Sound*, my primary intention was to give voice to Prince William Sound and its wild inhabitants. All too easily, place becomes mere backdrop for human drama. That's not what I wanted to write, nor what I felt needed to be written, but it's a strong magnet. As humans, we like to read about other humans. Early on, some readers, including a high-profile agent, wanted the book to be about the human story, with the Sound fading into setting. That was a suggestion I had to reject many times.

Oddly, I found the solution to giving voice while sitting in the dentist's chair, spaced out on nitrous oxide. Moments in the Sound floated to me in a series of images: three river otters playing in an upland pond; terns flying by at sunset, their bellies lit orange; fireweed gathered by a streambank, brilliant fuchsia lighting the land. I wrote these moments of being in present tense, as short prose pieces between longer narrative chapters.

And so I've come to rely on writing in present tense as another valuable cairn. I now write every first draft in present tense, sometimes changing to past tense in revision. This drops me right back in that place and time so my writing can more truthfully give voice. Most important, this helps me connect with the nonhuman world because that's where the rest of the world *always* is: in the present moment. There's no past, no future, just this present moment.

Still, it's tough to keep the nonhuman at the forefront when our understanding can be so limited. Simply calling an animal "he" or "she" rather than "it," using "who" instead of "what," gives agency. For an animal to become a primary character, he must become individualized. I'm working on a novel that has a polar bear as a character. It's not magical realism, so he doesn't talk and can't interact much, but there are ways of making him both representative of his species and a unique individual. A main character relates to him, spends time with him, notes his character and temperament in different situations, notes how he is and is not like other polar bears she observes. She learns about him through other humans who also spend time around him, as well as experts on polar bears. She imagines what life is like for him. And yet he remains a mystery, another nation.

The more I learn of the nonhuman world, the more aware I am of how we use language to simplify, degrade, and desacralize it. How often have we read the words *take, cull,* and *harvest* for *kill?* Language should reveal, not conceal. As a research assistant at the University of Alaska, I edited a report on the state's oil economy. Seeking to clarify, I used the word *extraction* rather than *production* because we're not creating oil; we're just pulling it from the ground. Still, the lead economist changed it back to *production.* I wasn't surprised, given industry standards, but I also haven't forgotten how one word shifted the perception of reality. Again, we must look to clarity of thinking and shedding cultural layers. Again, we must be aware of where we get our stories. We must depend on direct sensory experience.

In the crypt of London's St. Martin-in-the-Fields, I found a book called *Being a Beast*, in which Charles Foster describes his attempts to live, for a while, like a series of wild animals: badger, otter, fox, deer, swift. I bought it, then went upstairs into the church to listen to a Vivaldi concert, violin and viola music soaring to the vaulted ceilings as if not one note had ever before been issued into the world. I was surrounded by the beauty that humans can create, even as I held in my hands a book about the yearning to connect to the more-than-human.

I'd recently read another book, *Being Caribou*, about a couple's attempts to follow the Porcupine Caribou herd on its annual migration in the Canadian and Alaskan Arctic. I was struck by finding another account of humans trying to "be" another animal—by that desire, and its attempt, as flawed as it is, for we can never escape the human lens. In *Being Caribou*, much of the story concerns the very human needs of the couple—for their food drops, for shelter from the wind and snow and insects, for aching feet and sunburned faces. In one memorable scene, the author finally walks with the herd and has a moment of being, a PIE. But mostly, as with the charming *Being a Beast*, the book is about the writer's own very human struggles.

And yet this yearning is strong. It is lifelong: What child has not imagined herself another animal? It is vital: We must try to relate, to comprehend, even as nonhuman animals are disappearing from our grasp faster than we can name them. Because we as a society mostly know the more-than-human world through story, the stories we write are critically important. And never more so than now, in this time of great change across the planet.

Works Cited

Abram, David. 1996. *The Spell of the Sensuous: Perception and Language in a More-than-Human World.* New York: Pantheon.

Austin, Mary. 1903. *The Land of Little Rain.* New York: Houghton Mifflin.

Beston, Henry. 1928. *The Outermost House: A Year of Life on the Great Beach of Cape Cod.* New York: Doubleday.

Dillard, Annie. 1983. "Living Like Weasels." *Teaching a Stone to Talk.* New York: Harper Colophon.

Foster, Charles. 2016. *Being a Beast: An Intimate and Radical Look at Nature.* London: Profile Books.

Gornick, Vivian. 2001. *The Situation and the Story: The Art of Personal Narrative.* New York: Farrar, Straus and Giroux.

Haber, Gordon, and Marybeth Holleman. 2013. *Among Wolves: Gordon Haber's Insights into Alaska's Most Misunderstood Animal.* Fairbanks, Alaska: University of Alaska Press.

Heuer, Karsten. 2008. *Being Caribou: Five Months on Foot with an Arctic Herd.* Minneapolis: Milkweed Editions.

Holleman, Marybeth. 2004. *The Heart of the Sound: An Alaskan Paradise Found and Nearly Lost.* Lincoln, Nebraska: Bison Books.

Holleman, Marybeth. 1992. "A Reflection on Trumpeter Swans." *Searching the Land.* MFA Thesis, University of Alaska, Anchorage.

Primack, Gretchen. 2014. "The Greening of Literature: Eco-Fiction and Poetry to Enlighten and Inspire." Presentation at Association of Writers and Writing Programs Conference. Seattle, Washington. March 1.

Rogers, Pattiann. 1996. "What Among Heavens and Stars." *Orion Society Notebook*, vol. 2, no. 2.

Simpson, Sherry. 2013. *Dominion of Bears: Living with Wildlife in Alaska*. Lawrence, Kansas: University Press of Kansas.

Woolf, Virginia. 1985. *Moments of Being*. London: Harvest Books.

Giving Animals a Voice: Letters from an Ashland Deer

John Yunker

Animals talk. All around us, they converse and whisper and shout. But because they speak in different languages, we, like travelers in a foreign land, often tune out their voices, generalizing them into a background of bird calls, squirrel chirps, and dog barks.

But there are some of us, such as naturalists and writers, who do try to interpret these foreign languages.

Naturalists have devoted lifetimes to unlocking the secrets of the whale's sonar songs and the prairie dog's complex vocabulary. And they have slowly progressed, albeit paced by peer reviews and the scientific phobia of being accused of anthropomorphizing animals.

Writers are bound by no such restrictions. Writers are free to imagine, to speculate, to invent languages. Writers are bound only by the reader's suspension of disbelief. Writers give voices to animals in novels and short stories, in poems and picture books. And, as this essay illustrates, even through letters to the editor. What follows is a story of how I was inspired to give my own voice to a species that needed one in an ongoing, life-and-death drama taking pace in a small town in Oregon.

Backstory: Where Suburbs Meet Wilderness

Ashland is a small, southern Oregon town on the edge of the Klamath National Forest, one of the most ecologically diverse regions in the United States. So it's no surprise that the streets of Ashland are sometimes traversed not only by humans and cars but by bears, coyotes, mountain lions, and, most common of all, black-tailed deer.

Over the years deer have become so comfortable in Ashland that they have made it their home. It's hard to blame them. The town offers a plethora of food in the forms of lush landscaping and organic gardens, as well as a degree of protection from mountain lions (though not cars). And for many years, the human residents have been mostly accommodating of the neighborhood cervids.

But in the past seven years that I've lived in Ashland I've noticed a changing sentiment. Ashland is home to a growing number of people relocating from large urban areas, such as San Francisco, Portland, and Seattle. People who are not accustomed to seeing deer on their front lawns, let alone eating their front lawns. People who view such animals as a nuisance.

And a vocal number of people have begun to view deer as a threat.

Deer Attack!

In journalism, there is an aphorism: *If a dog bites a man, it is not news; if a man bites a dog, that is news.* In 2015, a handful of residents reported being "stalked" and "attacked" by deer, a story that quickly gathered national attention.

We don't know exactly what was behind these attacks, how severe they actually were, or even if they actually happened, as there were no reported hospital visits and no police reports. Naturalists generally agree that these "attacks" were simply the result of female deer protecting their young. A mother deer will cross the street to stand between a dog and her young, an act that is justifiably intimidating to humans. Just because a dog walker doesn't see fawns nearby doesn't mean they are not there. I, too, once encountered a mother deer who put herself between me and her fawns, approaching rather than walking away. In that case, I stopped and turned around. But sometimes people don't see the deer coming in time to react.

In the media, a chorus of voices began calling for a "culling" of the deer. I felt that something needed to be done in defense of these creatures I love sharing our town with. And I realized that amidst all the chatter, a critical voice was not being heard.

The voices of the deer themselves.

At the time of these complaints, the city was conducting controlled burns in the hills surrounding Ashland in an effort to minimize forest fires. But this, along with heavy mountain biking in the hills, was never talked about when people complained about all the deer in town.

So I undertook an anonymous (until now) letter-writing campaign taking on the voice of an "Ashland Deer." These letters were published in a free and widely read Ashland periodical, *Sneak Preview,* and generated significant reader response. Here is the first letter, published in July of 2015, from "the deer," written with the goal of giving the deer's perspective.

Letter from an Ashland Deer to the residents of Ashland,

It has come to my attention over the past year that a number of Ashland residents are unhappy with our presence in their yards and streets. Some have gone so far as to propose the culling (oh, let's not sugarcoat it: slaughtering) of deer.

True, we deer do enjoy your landscaping a bit too much. And, yes, we do not observe local traffic laws, something we're working on (a few additional deer crossing signs would certainly help). Some residents wonder why we don't simply return to our "home" up in the wilderness that surrounds the town.

I'm writing to tell you that we've tried. Trust me on this. But so far our efforts have been thwarted. Allow me to explain.

A few months ago, we spent a few evenings in the forest only to be awakened by humans setting brushfires all around us. We later learned that this was part of Ashland's ongoing "thinning" project, which, for the record, we support. But all this cutting and burning does make it rather difficult for us deer to settle in up there, wouldn't you think? And good luck finding something to eat amidst all that charred underbrush.

Nevertheless, I convinced a handful of fellow deer to give the woods one more try. After a bit of searching we found an uncharred section to settle down in, only to be terrorized as wave upon wave of mountain bikers descended upon us. Apparently, there was some sort of race going on, and I don't mind telling you that we felt safer dodging cars on the streets of Ashland than dodging bikers up on those hills.

For those humans who find deer a nuisance in Ashland, I simply wish to stress that we deer have similar thoughts regarding humans in our forests.

I sincerely hope that most residents do not support the killing of our kind. We know that the tourists love to see us—and, so I'm told, a good many locals. I ask that we all follow the wise instruction of a bumper sticker I often seen around town and "coexist."

Kindly yours,
An Ashland Deer

The Ashland Deer soon received letters in reply. In one letter, the author documented the "trauma" she suffered while walking her dog and accused the deer of "terrorizing" residents. Another letter writer suggested deer sterilization (a solution that has proven ineffective in other towns). What I found interesting was not just that people were responding to the deer, including addressing the deer directly, but that there was a great deal of passion behind their letters. Instead of a debate between two humans with the deer remaining voiceless, here was a debate between the human and the deer.

The Ashland Deer responded to the first round of comments, in the September 2015 issue, as follows:

Your Ashland Deer Again,

First, I wish to thank you for your thoughtful responses to my initial letter. Clearly, this is an issue that incites passions both for and against my species, your silent cohabitants.

To the president of the Ashland Woodland and Trails Association, I did not wish to imply that all mountain bikers drive dangerously. We deer do appreciate the efforts of the vast majority of Ashlanders and visitors to coexist with us in town as well as in the hills above town.

To the resident who lives in fear of a stalking, malicious deer, I sincerely apologize for your troubles. As with any species, there are always a few "bad apples." Trust me when I say that we deer are, by nature, keen to avoid humans. It is only when we're protecting our young that, well, our hormones can get the better of us.

But should all deer suffer from random killings or sterilization simply because a mother was aggressive in her efforts to protect her young? Should a rogue deer be used to justify terrorizing all deer? As one letter noted, more than 250 deer have died from car accidents from 2001 to 2011. Isn't this enough culling of our species?

Finally, to the resident who proposes bow hunting within city limits: Right now—perhaps thanks to Cecil the Lion—I am picturing a viral video of a deer with an arrow jutting from her bleeding neck, dazed and stumbling through an Oregon Shakespeare Festival Green Show.

Surely the wise business and tourism leaders of Ashland appreciate that people visit our beautiful town of Ashland to experience nature—not to escape from it. They visit to appreciate wildlife—not to see it slaughtered.

I understand that we deer are not universally loved or appreciated, but here in Ashland, we all live on the edge of a national forest. If Ashland were to one day lose its wildlife, it would lose so much more.

Peacefully yours,
Your Ashland Deer

As these letters were running back and forth, a number of residents rallied for the city to act, which resulted in a "Deer Summit" held later that year in the city council chambers.

At this standing-room-only meeting, the mayor claimed that he, too, had been "stalked" by a deer. A few local experts who had studied the deer issue for many years gave the consensus that sterilization was futile, as was the idea of killing deer; other deer would simply take their places.

But that didn't prevent more than a dozen residents from urging the city to undertake some sort of culling. As is the case with so much talk of killing animals, the details are often far messier than people would like to admit. Exactly how such a slaughter would be effected was unclear. Would all residents be required to stay inside while hunters roamed the streets with guns, or bows and arrows? This is why so much nastiness occurs when killing wildlife remains in the dark. We like to assume that hunters kill animals with one shot, that animals feel nothing. We don't want to think of deer wandering the streets with arrows in their necks, or missing legs, or bleeding on our sidewalks.

Fortunately, about a dozen residents spoke up in defense of the deer. For every woman who said she felt in danger walking the streets of Ashland, another woman spoke up saying she felt perfectly safe.

Two years later, I'm happy to report that no culling has been proposed. The city now posts warning signs when residents report being harassed by deer, and no-feeding signs have gone up as well. I don't believe the issue has gone away so much as hibernated as other, more pressing issues took priority.

But I do believe the deer articles made a difference—because the minute people begin addressing an animal the way one addresses a human, something changes in the discussion. Perhaps this is why those who resist the idea of animal rights are so quick to tell activists not to "humanize" animals.

What Other Species Can Write Letters to the Editor?

There is no reason that deer alone can wield a pen. Certainly other species that are often demonized, such as wolves, cougars, and bears, could dash off a letter or two. And I encourage anyone who faces deer conflicts—or any other human-wildlife conflict—in his or her town to copy these letters and reuse them as needed.

Humor May Succeed Where Facts Fail

The goal with these letters was to humanize the deer. When an animal has a voice, that animal feels significantly closer to us humans. Our companion animals speak to us, and more often than not, we know exactly what they're saying. If we can hear them—and enjoy their Facebook and Instagram pages—why not give voices to less popular species when it really matters?

Ultimately, I believe animal letters can help in activism. And they can be entertaining, both to write and to read. Our local *Sneak Preview* includes a regular feature at the back of the magazine, profiling a member of the community with a Q&A. Needless to say, our Ashland Deer did not want to be left out and answered the same questions the humans do for this feature. This profile was published a few months after the Deer Summit, in September of 2016:

> **Profile:** An Ashland Deer.
> **Birthplace:** Above the boulevard.
> **Birthdate:** I don't remember the exact date but it was dark, and the sky was clear.
> **Marital Status:** Still playing the field.
> **Tell us something about your organization and/or job:** I strive to visit Ashland's most lush lawns and gardens. I also enjoy posing for photographs as the tourists pass through town. I like to think of us as the unofficial ambassadors of Ashland.
> **How long have you lived in southern Oregon?** Ever since I was born.
> **Favorite movie:** Any movie but *Bambi* or *The Deer Hunter*.
> **Favorite play:** *Into the Woods.*
> **Favorite actor:** Joaquin Phoenix. He's a big fan of all animals.
> **Favorite actress:** Helen Mirren. She shared a

wonderful scene in *The Queen* with a member of my species.

Favorite TV show: *Downton Abbey.* Oh, how I yearn for those juicy gardens!

Favorite radio station: KSKQ.

Favorite book of all time: *Animal Farm.*

What book are you currently reading? I tend to read less during the busy summer months.

Favorite magazine: *Vegetarian Times.*

Favorite pet of all time: Any pet that is securely leashed.

Other than friends or family, what person do you admire most? The fine people who came to my defense at City Hall last fall. It's nice to know we deer have friends in high places.

What's the first thing you turn to when you read a daily newspaper? Weather forecast. I like to have the chance to take cover rather than get stuck in a sudden downpour.

Favorite part of the *Sneak Preview*: The letters.

Favorite hobbies: Chewing my cud. Also, looking into the windows of people's homes at night and catching the latest episode of *Game of Thrones.*

Favorite Beatle and/or Beatle song: "We Can Work it Out."

Favorite local restaurants: Lithia Park, and the median along Siskiyou Boulevard.

What would you do if you won $10 million in the lottery? Buy a few dozen of Ashland's finest homes and turn them into affordable housing, and take down all the deer fences.

What is the most important thing you learned as a child? Look both ways before crossing the road.

What person or event had the biggest impact on your life? My mother. When I still had my spots she told me that if I was going to make it in this town I had to stand my ground around dogs but also know when to run for it.

Proudest achievement: Getting to those sunflowers on Gresham Street.

Favorite thing about Ashland: So many organic gardens. And so many kind and tolerant people who don't mind when we nibble our way through.

At the time these pieces were published, I had not revealed myself as the writer, and I listened to people discuss the topic at cafés and at happy hours. I was glad people were talking about the deer in a way that they hadn't before—in a way that allowed for the animal to, finally, have a voice. Whether it's a letter to the editor or a profile that reveals a little bit of life in someone else's shoes, lending our voices to the animals takes us further down the path toward mutual understanding and—I hope—peaceful coexistence.

No One Mourns an Unnamed Animal: Why Naming Animals Might Help Save Them

Midge Raymond

When I volunteered to help with a penguin census at the Punta Tombo colony in the Patagonia region of Argentina, among the thousands of birds I counted, one of them stood out—and I still think of him more than ten years later. His name is Turbo—so named because he'd inexplicably built a nest under a turbo truck instead of within a burrow, like the other penguins of his species—and instead of looking for a mate, he preferred to hang out with the researchers.

Turbo has been tagged by scientists with a metal band, along with thousands of other birds in the colony. Yet Turbo also has a name, making him a local personality, while the other tagged birds in the colony have only five-digit numbers to identify them, making them nothing more than data. *Anthropomorphism*, the practice of projecting human qualities onto nonhuman animals, is often viewed pejoratively by the scientific community. But as a writer, not a scientist, I'm far more interested in character than in numbers. And since my time at Punta Tombo, whenever I receive updates on the colony, I look first for Turbo's name, for confirmation of his return from his months at sea.

Unlike humans, animals don't come into this world and receive a name, at least not in any human language. It took a non-scientist, Jane Goodall, to challenge conventions when it came to studying animal behavior; by naming chimpanzees instead of numbering them, she was able to live among them and observe them like no researcher before her ever had. She observed the chimp she named David Greybeard making and using tools. She witnessed an adolescent chimpanzee, Spindle, adopting an orphan named Mel. And when the mother chimp she named Flo died in 1972, *The London Times* printed an obituary.

When we give an animal a name, we give it an identity, an individuality that sets it apart from the rest of its nameless species. And, in doing so, we often can't help but develop an emotional attachment to these named creatures. This is why zoos and sanctuaries name their animals, and why, increasingly, wild animals whose species need attention are finding followers and sympathizers. When Cecil the Lion, a well-known and beloved resident of Hwange National Park, was killed by an American dentist last July, the world was outraged, and Cecil's death highlighted the endangered status of certain species of lions, the cruelty of trophy hunting, and the practice of raising lions for hunting.

Yet Cecil was just one of many. It took his death—and the

fact that he had a name—to raise the world's consciousness, to give a face to the lions of Africa. In a similar fashion, Lonesome George, the last of his species of Galápagos tortoise, who died in 2012, reminds us all of the fragility of these islands and of their endangered animals. Migaloo, the Australian humpback whale, is known not only for being a rare albino whale but also draws attention to issues facing whales and oceans worldwide.

That writers name animals to give them equal weight as characters is nothing new, and is especially common in children's literature—we all remember Charlotte and Wilbur, Stuart Little, the rats of NIMH. In adult literature, however, animals are more rarely seen as main characters. In *Animal Farm*, for example, the animal characters are allegorical rather than truly animal—and yet in more recent fiction, such as Garth Stein's *The Art of Racing in the Rain* and Gwyn Hyman Rubio's *Love and Ordinary Creatures*, the dog and cockatoo characters, respectively, are meant to be just what they are: animals.

In my novel, *My Last Continent*, I gave a name to a penguin who plays an important role in the story. He's called Admiral Byrd, after an explorer admired by the human character who names him. That this penguin needed a name other than "the gentoo" or "the penguin" or "the bird" was based not only on his importance to the characters in the novel but his importance to me, as the author. I wanted Admiral Byrd to represent all the penguins in my fictional world, who in turn represent all the penguins in the real one.

Humans have a complicated relationship with animals, though, and naming them—in literature or in life—doesn't always mean saving them. In 4-H clubs around the country, animals raised by children and called by name are sold for slaughter by the pound. Oregon's first confirmed wolf since

1947 is called Journey but is more commonly known as OR-7. Even animals at the shelter where I volunteer, though they have names, are identified primarily by number.

New York Times editor Philip B. Corbett wrote in a February 2, 2016, article that the *Times* uses "person" pronouns "only for animals who have been given a name, or in cases where the sex of the animal is specified. Otherwise, we stick with 'it' and 'that' or 'which.'" In other words, the *Times* is about grammar, not about a point of view. But for those of us who do write with a point of view, names and pronouns are important.

We live in an era in which so many species are in decline that it's impossible to keep count. From the Malayan tiger to the New Zealand sea lion to the Galápagos penguin, the numbers of endangered animals are staggering. Yet if every species has a named representative or two, we civilians might get to know who will be lost on a more personal level—and we might be more inspired to help them all.

Scientists can continue to resist anthropomorphism—but this won't save the animals, or make the rest of the world pay attention. Yet if we give these animals names, if we look at them as more than data, we might care more deeply. The more we humanize animals, the more human we become.

Turbo the penguin is now eleven years old. He's still single, preferring the company of humans to his own species. In the fall, I'll eagerly await news of his return to the colony—where he will choose to build his nest, whether he'll still be a bachelor or will finally settle down. The data tells us a story—but Turbo himself tells the same story in an entirely different way. And as long as Turbo shows up each year, I feel as though there is hope for all of these birds.

Part IV:
Writers Change the World

Are You Willing?

Sangamithra Iyer

One autumn evening in New York, I was invited as a guest speaker to a college class on food writing taught by my friend Lisa Freedman. At the beginning of each class, Lisa shares a poem with her students. Since I was to be discussing writing about animals, Lisa chose Mary Oliver's poem "Lead."

"Here is a story to break your heart," Oliver's poem begins. "Are you willing?"

These opening lines are both a warning and an invitation. Oliver prepares her readers for what they are about to learn and also requests their participation. In those two lines she has grabbed her readers' attention and secured their investment in the story that follows.

Oliver then tells a tragic tale of dying loons intended to open—not close— the reader's heart to the world.

This is the crux of what many of us who write about animals want to do—will hearts open to change. I can't say I was successful that night in our discussions about food and animals. The students were reading Jonathan Safran Foer's book *Eating Animals* at the time and were in that vulnerable, uncomfortable phase of reconciling the realities of animal lives and their own. One student read her work. The writing was strong, and it shared a common narrative used by many prominent writers in prominent publications when discussing animals consumed for food: A writer learns the truth about where food comes from. A writer wrestles with it. There is tension between the belly and the brain. The belly ultimately wins. "But it tastes so good," the writer laments, throwing up her arms in futility. The ending is supposed to be humorous and self-deprecating, but it is too easy. The reader and writer are let off the hook. The heart isn't broken open, just mildly bruised with a shield over it.

How can we move beyond this narrative when it comes to writing about animals? What can we learn from this place of discomfort and how to transcend it? At the time, I was also embarking on a project to edit *Satya: The Long View*, a book-length anniversary edition of *Satya* magazine, which focused on the intersections between animals, environmentalism, and social justice. I began to see Oliver's poem as a guide toward understanding writing that makes unwilling readers willing when it comes to approaching the subject of animals. As a reader, writer, and editor, I would like to share some insights for writers to consider when writing animal literature, either fiction or nonfiction.

Here Is a Story

The challenge of reaching unwilling readers goes back centuries. Animal rights pioneer Henry Salt, in his 1886 essay "A Plea for Vegetarianism," also laments the difficulty of advocating for animals:

It is a mournful fact that when people have no wish to understand a thing, they can generally contrive to misunderstand it; and the hopelessness of pleading with those who will not or cannot comprehend is one of the first lessons learnt by Food Reformers, as indeed, by reformers of all kinds.

But Salt cleverly begins his essay by disarming the reader. He opens with a confession—that he is a vegetarian and that "this is rather a formidable admission to make, for a Vegetarian is still regarded, in ordinary society, as little better than a madman, and may consider himself lucky if he has no worse epithets applied to him than humanitarian, sentimentalist, crotchet-monger, fanatic, and the like." There is nothing the reader can call him that he hasn't already been called.

Salt continues: "A man who leaves off eating flesh will soon find that his friends and acquaintances look on him with strange and wondering eyes; his life is invested with a mysterious interest; his death is an event which is regarded as by no means distant or improbable ... "

But then he implores that "it will be worth our while to inquire if there be really such great absurdity in the idea of not eating flesh, or it be possible that the Vegetarians have reason on their side ... " Salt's technique is to first acknowledge his critics, and then skillfully refute them.

In his *Satya* essay, "Vegan for Life?!," Eric Weiss follows Salt's example in addressing a recent phenomenon—the rise of the ex-vegans. Weiss also begins with a confession: "People are often surprised to find out I'm vegan ... I'm a big guy, six feet tall and pushing three hundred pounds." He continues, "So I may not look the part, but I do care about and respect animals. So much so that I haven't eaten their flesh or paid someone to steal their milk or eggs for me for over 21 years." Weiss notes how this is remarkable only in relation to some of his peers, who have gone back to eating animal products. He then asks, "[H]ow did these same people wake up one day and decide well, I think I'll kill me some animals today?"

Again, like Salt, Weiss lays out the common explanations and refutes them one by one. For example, to the excuse "I'm just listening to my body," Weiss responds, "Did you ever think that maybe your body is a selfish asshole?" But before the reader can be offended, he quips, "Mine is. It demands chocolate and cake and bread and sugar all fucking day. It wants to sit around and watch television instead of going to the gym and doing the dishes."

Weiss and Salt both use humor and self-deprecation in their essays. It works for them and the animals because it doesn't deflect from the seriousness of what is at stake. The writer can joke about himself but in a way that is not at the expense of the animals. It is instead a way to infuse logic and reasoning to counter the normalization of violence against animals.

I Tell You This

Writing about animals in a way that challenges rather than accepts societal norms is a radical act. Any radical act is often met with resistance. Why are hearts reluctant to fully open? In her essay in *Cultural Anthropology*, "Witness: Humans, Animals, and the Politics of Becoming," ethnographer Naisargi Dave recounts a story of a woman telling her she could never volunteer at an animal shelter because she was "deathly afraid of caring too much." Dave then asks, "Is any other politics, I wonder, constrained by such a mortal fear of caring too much, of the heart bursting, the skin thinning, of not being able to rest again?" This encounter resembles conversations animal advocates may have with acquaintances who cover their ears and kindly request, "Please don't tell me. I don't want to know."

In my interview with Dave in *Satya: The Long View*, I asked her to unpack this fear. She talked about concepts she calls the "descent into obligation" or the "tyranny of obligation." "The question becomes, once I have opened myself up beyond the ethical boundaries to which I had become accustomed, based on what criteria will I close the circle again? Once I care, how can I not care?"

Opting out of caring becomes a self-defense mechanism, a way to protect the heart. As a writer and editor, I wonder how understanding these fears can help us reach the reader who reads with her hands over her eyes.

A writer can choose to "write into" this fear. For example, in Karen Joy Fowler's novel *We Are All Completely Beside Ourselves*, the animal-rights activist Lowell tells his sister Rosemary about the violence against animals he's witnessed and the burdens of sharing it. "'The world runs,' Lowell said, 'on the fuel of this endless fathomless misery. People know it, but they don't mind what they don't see. Make them look and they mind, but you're the one they hate, because you're the one that made them look.'"

"We ought to be able to act as each moment dictates or invites, but instead, we tend to feel that if we do something, we must therefore do everything, and if we cannot, then we might as well do nothing," Dave further explained in her interview in *Satya*. Writing is one way of focusing on the moment, and our characters can choose to do what they think is right in that particular moment. For example, in his nonfiction book *Zeitoun*, Dave Eggers recounts the story of

Abdulrahman Zeitoun in the aftermath of Hurricane Katrina. In the days after the storm, Zeitoun stayed back to help his city, paddling along the flooded streets in his canoe, trying to assist people in need. But he could not exclude animals from his consideration. "He thought of the animals. The squirrels, the mice, rats, frogs, possums, lizards. All gone. Millions of animals drowned." Zeitoun then remembered the dogs. "He rested his paddle on his lap, coasting, trying to place the pets he'd heard crying in the dark." Over the next few days he located abandoned dogs and brought them food. "It was one of the strangest aspects of this in-between time—after the storm but before anyone had returned to the city—the presence of these thousands of left-behind animals," Zeitoun reflected. But one day he found a number of animals shot dead, and he couldn't understand why.

> There were so many boats in the city. It would only take a moment to take them aboard and set them loose anywhere. But perhaps something had changed irrevocably. That this was considered a sane or even humane option signaled that reason had left this place.

Telling the story of the animals after the hurricane did not detract from the other horrors of the situation but rather helped create a fuller picture.

The myth of the "tyranny of obligation" and the normalization of animal violence are related. Dave contends that is how normality retains itself. In reality, our decent into obligation happens more organically and freely. Writers can show on the page how a character's thinking about animals is an evolving process. In her *Satya* essay "Gateway Dog,"

Lisa Freedman writes about her shift in thinking after she adopted her dog Jenkins. When Jenkins accidentally ingests rat poison on the streets of Coney Island, Freedman learns that if she had not found speedy treatment, the rodenticide would have caused Jenkins to die from internal bleeding. "It was undeniably cruel to expose Jenkins to this; why had I never thought of poisoning rats and mice as cruel, too?" Later in the essay, she describes coming across an injured seagull along the beach. "My heart hurt and my pulse raced the way it does when I pass the aftermath of a car crash. This is crazy, feeling all this concern for a seagull while I continue to buy and eat chicken and beef, not to mention yogurt and cheese (products of realities I still struggle to remember these days as I work myself toward veganism). I vowed to stop eating meat." Adopting a dog was her gateway to these realizations. "Jenkins taught me to expand my concept of justice and to care about birds and cows and rats and all who can't make demands for themselves." Freedman guides the reader in her thought process and the connections she is making along the way.

In another *Satya* essay, "I Brake for Turtles," Wende Crow poetically explores her own awakening into the lives of animals. "I cannot decide whether I want to grow wings or roots, but I know I want to grow," she concludes. By choosing the word *grow*, Crow reminds us that our hearts are always expanding. With wings or roots, the descent into obligation in reality is not tyrannical but liberating.

To Break Your Heart

In *The Politics of the Brokenhearted*, Parker Palmer writes, "If our hearts are to be broken open rather than apart, we must claim periods of what Taoists call *wu-wei*—literally 'purposeless wandering,' or creative nonaction, *making space within and around ourselves so that conflict and confusion can settle and a deeper wisdom emerge."*

How can we apply this practice to writing about animals? How as writers do we create spaces in our work to allow the reader to process the uncomfortable and emerge with a deeper wisdom that defies the initial response of avoidance or futility?

In *Eating Animals*, Jonathan Safran Foer purposely takes some time before delving head-on into the subject matter of his book. He begins with a story about his grandmother, family, and tradition. Foer then has a chapter devoted to his dog George, before turning his attention to the animals killed for food. His gradual entry into the subject matter and the juxtaposition of these pieces act as a sort of *wu-wei*, slowly guiding the reader into new territory.

Maxine Hong Kingston, in her memoir *The Woman Warrior: Memoirs of a Girlhood among Ghosts*, notes how her heart could differentiate between the animals slaughtered for food and those we call companions. "I could feel a wooden door inside of me close. I had learned on the farm that I could stop loving animals raised for slaughter. And I could start loving them immediately when someone said, 'This one is a pet,' freeing me and opening the door." Kingston observes that loving animals is "freeing," while suppressing that love is confining. Language has the power to open and close this door. Through words and narrative, writers have the ability to convey animals as subjects, not objects; beings, not pests.

One of the best arguments against zoos that I've seen came from the fictional talking gorilla in Daniel Quinn's book *Ishmael: An Adventure of the Mind and Spirit*.

> [I]n Africa I was a member of a family—a sort of family that people of your culture haven't known

for thousands of years. If gorillas were capable of such an expression, they would tell you that their family is like a hand, of which they are fingers. They are fully aware of being a family but are very little aware of being individuals. Here in the zoo there were other gorillas—but there was no family. Five severed fingers do not make a hand.

This closing line has stayed with me as a compelling case against captivity. And one of the most compelling cases for animals that I've seen came from a man held captive in Guantánamo Bay. In "A Handful of Walnuts," an excerpt published in *Granta* from his memoir, *The General*, Ahmed Errachidi reveals the disturbing set of experiences that led to his detention in Guantánamo Bay and how he coped with captivity. It was this passage about "the visitors," that drew me to the piece:

> Visitors would come three times a day after every meal. They would come by the dozen, and I would wait eagerly for them. I would sit with them, thoroughly enjoying their company. I spent long hours with them, and yet did not get bored. They would come and give us hope that life had not come to a halt.

Errachidi is describing a community of ants:

> I secretly saved food for them in a corner. If the guards saw them they would either spray them with pesticide or crush them beneath their military boots. I would get angry, and shout at

them, "Do not the ants have a right to life? They do not trouble you so why do you have to kill them?" When the soldiers found out that we fed the ants, they punished us by cutting our rations. That didn't stop me from keeping ants in my cell. I observed them and studied their way of life every day.

Errachidi describes how he watched the ants, left peanut shells for them, and gave them droplets of sweet tea. When the guards came, he would blow at them, signaling them to disperse, so they would not be crushed by a shoe. Errachidi is able to tell a larger story of Guantánamo Bay—the injustice and inhumanity of it as well as these rare moments of beauty and kindness—by sharing this small, intimate act of thoughtful observation of ants. While the detainee and the ant are often misunderstood, Errachidi's observations bring renewed understanding to both.

So It Can Never Again be Closed

In *Satya: The Long View*, I share this anecdote about Mohandas K. Gandhi's journey in 1888 from India to London to study law. He arrived in England carrying a promise to his mother that he would not eat meat while in Europe. At the age of nineteen, Gandhi was both a reluctant vegetarian and a reluctant meat eater. Like many of his young peers, he thought it was the Indian's duty to eat meat to conquer the oppressor. He had come to believe that meat was the source of strength for the British, and vegetarianism was India's weakness. Gandhi described his early attempts at meat eating as a teenager in his autobiography, *The Story of My Experiments with Truth*. This carnivorous experiment left him with nightmares of a live goat bleating inside him. But perhaps what kept Gandhi vegetarian as a young man was the fear of disappointing his parents.

Abstaining from meat in London proved to be challenging. The young Gandhi subsisted on porridge and too few slices of bread (he was too shy to ask for more bread than what was offered to him). One evening he stumbled upon the Central Vegetarian Restaurant on Farrington Street. "The sight of it filled me with the same joy that a child feels on getting a thing after his own heart," Gandhi wrote in his autobiography. There, he consumed his "first hearty meal" since his arrival in England, and discovered an essay that would change his life.

In the display case of the restaurant was a copy of Salt's "A Plea for Vegetarianism," which Gandhi then purchased for a shilling and devoured with as much delight as his meal. It was in this moment that Gandhi recommitted to vegetarianism by choice and not out of familial duty. He would later come to believe vegetarianism was a key strength—not weaknesses—in the effort to fight for Indian independence.

By laying out the deep set of challenges associated with advocating for animals where cruelty was the norm, Salt's writings offered solidarity to those questioning this kind of societal violence, and became a call for action, for at least one significant reader, rather than an excuse to retreat.

I love imagining Gandhi discovering Salt in London—that chance encounter with words on the page, which sparks a connection, nurtures compassion, and spurs action. Such a moment inspired the soon-to-be activist Gandhi to cut his teeth in writing and organizing for the London Vegetarian Society. There, his colleagues introduced him to other works that continued to shape his thinking and provided the foundation for his future activism.

I tell you this to remind you that animal-rights literature

can indeed change the world. It already has.

Works Cited

Crow, Wende. 2016. "I Brake for Turtles." *Satya: The Long View.*

Dave, Naisargi. 2014. "Witness: Humans, Animals, and the Politics of Becoming." *Cultural Anthropology* 29, no. 3.

Eggers, Dave. 2009. *Zeitoun.* San Francisco: McSweeney's.

Errachidi, Ahmed. 2011. "A Handful of Walnuts." *Granta 116: Ten Years Later.*

Foer, Jonathan Safran. 2009. *Eating Animals.* New York: Little, Brown and Company.

Fowler, Karen Joy. 2013. *We Are All Completely Beside Ourselves.* New York: G. P. Putnam's Sons.

Freedman, Lisa. 2016. "Gateway Dog." *Satya: The Long View.*

Gandhi, Mohandas K. 1957. *Gandhi An Autobiography: The Story of My Experiments with Truth.* Boston: Beacon Press.

Iyer, Sangamithra. 2016. "The Ethnography of Activism: The *Satya* Interview with Naisargi Dave." *Satya: The Long View.*

———. 2016. "The Long View: Reading, Writing and Eating as Radical Acts." *Satya: The Long View.*

Kingston, Maxine Hong. 1989. *The Woman Warrior: Memoirs of a Girlhood among Ghosts.* New York: Vintage Books.

Oliver, Mary. 2005. "Lead." *New and Selected Poems, vol. 2.* Boston: Beacon Press.

Palmer, Parker. 2005. *The Politics of the Brokenhearted: On Holding the Tensions of Democracy.* Kalamazoo, MI: Feltzer Institute.

Quinn, Daniel. 1995. *Ishmael: An Adventure of the Mind and Spirit.* New York: Bantam Books.

Salt, Henry. 1886. "A Plea for Vegetarianism." *A Plea for Vegetarianism and Other Essays.* Manchester, UK: Manchester Vegetarian Society.

Weiss, Eric. 2016. "Vegan for Life?!" *Satya: The Long View.*

With a Hope to Change Things:
An Exploration of the Craft of Writing about Animals with the Founders of *Zoomorphic* Magazine

Alex Lockwood

In his new book, *The War Against Animals*, Dinesh Wadiwel suggests our primarily exploitative relationship with animals will change only when we create "spaces of truce" in society where we can relate differently to those with whom we share this planet. The thrust of Wadiwel's argument is that as humans we have, in regard to animals, overwhelmingly created institutions and spaces of violence rather than of kindness. What's worse is that we don't even realize this; the ways we organize our means of living generally don't allow for us to see violence against animals *as* violence—and certainly not as a war.

A space of truce is, writes Wadiwel, a place where different species can come together and create new connections, perhaps friendships, even relations of love and care. To create such alternative spaces for truce between human and nonhuman species calls, however, for a radical change in the practices of humans, who have colonized the majority of Earth's spaces for our own benefit. Part of this process is to open up spaces for our current ways of knowing animals to be challenged, and new forms of connection to be proposed and shared.

Zoomorphic magazine is one of these spaces. Launched in 2015, it was first an online magazine and is now also in print, featuring writing in celebration and defense of wild animals. It was established by Susan Richardson and James Roberts, two writers who have dedicated their practices, and much of their personal lives, to championing a space in which writers from around the world can share attempts to reconfigure how we perceive nonhuman animals and our entanglements with them—indeed, with animals' own entanglements with each other, outside of the human-centered view.

I first interviewed Susan and James after the launch of their first issue, sitting in a public park in the city of Cardiff, capital of Wales, on a blustery but warm summer's day after the two of them had conducted a *Zoomorphic* editorial meeting. They were both enthused by the reaction toward their venture, and keen to see it grow and shape the writing landscape for animals. I have followed *Zoomorphic* since, through seven issues and the publication of more than 150 writers. *Zoomorphic* has helped support a community of practice able to write, read, and share in the craft of writing about animals in more animal than anthropocentric ways. This has been critical to the way in which the project has developed.

I caught up again with Susan and James to see how the project has shifted and changed shape—a natural development for a publication interested and involved with the zoopoetics of wild animals. In both conversations, we explored the "macro" work of establishing an animal-centric space of truce for new writing, and the "micro" work of the individual acts of writing craft, technique, and imaginative leaps that shape and expand the animal-centric ethos of such a space. This essay is drawn from these interviews and follow-up conversations, the study of their books, and writing published in *Zoomorphic*. The value of *Zoomorphic* is, I argue, as a "space of truce," able to foster new ways of thinking about species relations as well as to offer insight into the practices of contemporary writers, exploring the craft skills, techniques, and imaginative ideas of *why* we write about nonhuman animals, and *how* we can better write of their extinctions and losses, as well as the celebration of animal-centric poetry and literature.

Susan Richardson is a poet and the author of three collections, her most recent being *skindancing* (Cinnamon Press), infused with myth, animal voice, and shapeshifting. She has worked with a number of environmental and animal organizations, including hosting bee-writing workshops for Friends of the Earth and serving as poet in residence for the World Animal Day action and for the Marine Conservation Society, for whom she is writing a new collection. James Roberts is an essayist, writer, and graphic designer, and author of the children's book *The Man in the Mountain* (Sea Campion), a story that combines old Welsh myth with the themes of contemporary species loss, especially of the decline in bird life as witnessed by James around his home in the Welsh Brecon Beacons.

Alex Lockwood: It's nice to reconnect with you both again. In what ways has *Zoomorphic* moved on since its inception?

Susan Richardson: The most obvious way is that it's no longer solely a digital literary publication. We published our first print anthology at the end of 2016: *Driftfish*, a marine species–themed anthology of poetry and prose. We've also started to curate public events such as exhibitions, live performances, and readings and writing workshops, all as a means of trying to reach out to more people with our animal-centric approach. Recently, we collaborated with the ONCA Centre for Arts and Ecology in Brighton to create, in their gallery space, a marine wildlife–themed exhibition featuring an installation of diving seabirds, paintings, and digital audio poetry, plus an evening of live performance to mark *Driftfish*'s launch.

We've also started offering prose and poetry workshops on such themes as wildlife writing and animal language in both England and Wales. I tend to take responsibility for the workshop side of things and am especially enjoying developing the animal language workshops, encouraging participants to experiment with speaking seal, writing owl, and translating wolf into human!

James Roberts: My original idea for the magazine was to be able to work with nature writers, poets, conservationists, and scientists—for the magazine to be a shared space for stories about wild animals. We have published articles by all of the above, plus pieces by wilderness guides, explorers, academics, philosophers, etc. Because we are digitally based, we have been able to reach out to people who would have been impossible to reach through print. Very recently we have begun publishing in a biweekly rather than an issue-based format, and I am hoping this year to be able to involve the magazine with a conservation initiative in the UK, working with shepherds, wildlife NGOs, and landowners.

AL: Can you tell us a little bit about where the idea for *Zoomorphic* came from?

SR: About eight years ago, I chose to forego all writing and teaching opportunities that didn't directly respond to the urgent issue of environmental destruction and, especially, biodiversity loss and species-level extinction. At the time, I was writing about a wide variety of different subjects and teaching a broad range of themed writing workshops and courses, but I felt I could no longer justify producing and teaching writing that didn't have an ecological/animal-centric impulse behind it. It felt like an exciting decision but also quite scary, as it meant I had to give up a lot of regular teaching, and I didn't know if there'd be enough work opportunities that would allow me to focus solely on the ecological. Happily, though, work has been plentiful, and I'm really grateful to have been involved in so many wonderful projects, *Zoomorphic* being one of them.

JR: That's the decision I also effectively made. I'd got to the point where I couldn't write about anything else except animals and the environment because it upsets me all of the time. I've got animals around me everywhere I go, all my life, and I've got young children, and I want them to have the same experiences I've had.

AL: What about your own work in this time? Are there new practices that have enabled you to deepen your responses in celebration and defense of animals, either in writing, or other ways?

SR: I've been working on my fourth collection, *Words the Turtle Told Me*, during this time. It's grown out of my poetry residency with the Marine Conservation Society, working specifically on their Thirty Threatened Species project. I've been both writing poetry and running poetry workshops, encouraging others to write poetry about endangered marine creatures, ranging from iconic species (such as the Atlantic puffin) to lesser-known animals (such as the frilled shark). During the residency period I've opted to take a range of courses, from the scientific (otter ecology, cetacean biology) to the more intuitive (telepathic animal communication). I've also felt the need to try to do something constructive and practical about the global marine litter problem that causes the deaths of so many marine creatures, so have committed to doing a weekly (or almost weekly!) beach clean. All of these things have had an impact on my writing about animals over the past couple of years.

JR: I've barely had the time. I would say that reading so much work from other parts of the world has made me focus a lot more on my own square mile. The degradation of the environment has led to an impoverishment here, in our little patch of Welsh upland, that needs addressing urgently. Now that the magazine is a little more established I'm getting more time to think about other projects, and my work will be focused on using my skills to engage local people with the surrounding wild community. What comes over when editing a publication like *Zoomorphic* is that you engage people better through stories, rather than theories, politics, and regulations.

AL: Has your editorship of the project and your nurturing of a community of writers shifted your thoughts on what animal-centric writing is/could be?

JR: Yes, definitely. Some writers who send work in are only able to write about themselves; the number of pieces I've received about the death of a loved one told metaphorically through the arrival or disappearance of an animal ... Writers need to focus outward, beyond themselves, beyond their own species. Spend time with dogs, cats, horses, etc., and find out what makes them totally different to other dogs, cats, horses. Watch sparrows warring in the park. If you find a slug in the garden, don't squash it—observe the way it feels its way carefully from one grass blade to the next, its whole body a sensing organ more in tune with its surroundings than a human being could ever be. Follow wader tracks across a beach and try to work out what the bird was searching for. Basically get outside of your own head. There is a line from a poem by Robert Bringhurst that is pinned to my wall: "Love means love of the thing sung, not of the song or the singing."

AL: What have been the most exciting and stimulating elements of the work you've published that illuminate the craft of writing about animals?

SR: I'm always excited by the sheer volume of poetry submissions I receive: It's heartening to be regularly reminded of the fact that so many people in so many different countries are committed to producing animal-centric writing, as this doesn't often filter through into the mainstream poetry world. I also much enjoyed co-editing our themed issue for World Animal Day 2015—we wanted to focus on animal welfare as well as endangered animals for that issue and received a number of wonderful (by which I mean honest, unflinching, and skillfully crafted) submissions from writers, especially in the US and Canada, whose work I hadn't come across before.

JR: The most exciting element of the project has been working with young people who do not see themselves as writers but have a story to tell. They have mostly been young conservationists working on their first projects, and they still have a deep passion for their work. I have been able to help them to tell their stories, and I don't think they would have been published elsewhere very easily, due to their lack of a track record. Their stories have been by far the most widely read of anything we've published, which is very satisfying. I want the magazine to be a space for stories and not just writers. I really love how poets and scientists can work together. Poetry creates a feeling, a deeper connection, a space around it that you're sucked into, but at the same time the more scientific writing can bring you to the world, the worldview of other people. The scientific knowledge comes from people who know those things are happening on the ground, which poets aren't necessarily going to know about.

SR: The two worlds [arts and science] are sadly often so far apart. Yet I've met quite a number of scientists, most recently when I've been running writing workshops for conservation organizations, who are craving new ways to share their work. "We've got all this important information," they say, referring to climate-change research, perhaps, or some new wildlife conservation project, "but how can we communicate it to the public in a more creative, accessible way?" My belief is that poetry, especially, is key here—it can be so very effective in inspiring shifts in perception and creating new patterns of thought in a reader or audience member, which can ultimately lead to behavior change.

AL: What relationships do you have with other animals? Are they relationships that you are able to or feel comfortable sharing in your writing?

SR: I have a very close relationship with my dog, Hooper—he's only appeared occasionally in my published writing but has lolloped through the pages of my journal for almost ten years now. As for wild animals, I regularly walk a stretch of the Pembrokeshire coast and am very aware of the whole network of animals, from kestrels to choughs to porpoises, that I see there most days. I've had a few spine-tingling eye-to-eye encounters with both the resident male and female kestrels and feel very privileged that they both accept my presence, apparently completely comfortable even if I'm standing right next to their fence perch. I also do weekly Atlantic grey seal-watching and -monitoring at a local beach, and love following the annual rhythm of their lives from pregnancy to pupping to molting. My next book is going to be seal-themed, and those from my local area will feature prominently.

JR: I've spent my whole life surrounded by animals. Usually dogs and horses but also the various creatures that live in my large and very overgrown garden. There are currently five birds' nests within a few meters of my bedroom window; a small flock of house sparrows lives almost permanently in the garden, as well as dunnocks and various tits and finches. There is a large rookery just down the hill, a wood with buzzards and red kites, cows and sheep staring over the back fence. I see all of these as close relationships. But when I was younger I spent a long period in East Africa, and ever since, my view of my own square mile is that it is hugely depleted. And now, having lived in the same place for a number of years, what I also notice is that the depletion is continuing at an accelerating pace. The reduction in numbers of wild species is not just a statistic on a website or in a journal. It is all around me, a slowly growing silence. Years ago there were lapwings on the hill—now there are none, and the curlew are almost gone. So for all the joy of sharing a life with animals, I also have a deep sense of loss, and these two things interact in almost everything I write.

AL: Can you tell me a bit more about your engagement with myths and indigenous creation stories, and how integral they are as a part of your practice of writing about animals?

SR: My third collection of poetry, *skindancing*, is entirely themed around human-animal/nonhuman-animal metamorphosis, and it explores both our intimacy with, and alienation from, the wild and our animal selves—the animal without and the animal within. My sources of inspiration include shapeshifting tales from a number of different cultures, from Inuit to Celtic, Native American to Norse. The more reading and research I did while writing this collection, the more it became evident that in our Western story tradition, there are very few positive representations of human–animal shapeshifting; the process of transformation usually comes about as a result of a curse or as a form of punishment. By contrast, in many indigenous stories, transformation into a nonhuman animal is something to be embraced and celebrated. It may be the means by which a character extricates herself from an unpleasant or difficult situation, for example. For me, this contrast came to symbolize the dysfunctional relationship with both the animal within and the wider animal world that exists in Western cultures.

Many of the poems in *skindancing* were also inspired by my experience of, and training in, shamanic journeying and shamanic trance dance—this has had a significant influence on my work over the past five years by opening up new, intuitive routes into the poetry-writing process, mainly through enabling me to develop relationships with Power Animals.

AL: Do you have any tips for those who want to move toward producing more animal-centric writing?

SR: At the moment, I'm very interested in exploring ways of stimulating engagement, through writing, with animals who may be less accessible and/or with whom humans find it more challenging to empathize (for example, some of the cold-blooded, deep underwater creatures about whom I've been writing during my Marine Conservation Society residency). I've been experimenting with language, metaphor, and the animal voice (sometimes in radical ways, sometimes less so) and would love to encourage other writers to explore in this way, too.

JR: I really love reading reports, a lot of science. What amazed me recently was a seal report done on the island of Skomer.

They thought the seal colony there was about eighty or ninety seals, and the scientists thought they were resident but found some of the seals were traveling to Cornwall and back in twenty-four hours. They found a pup that had swum all the way around the UK coast and ended up in the Shetland Isles. So young, too! I get a lot of the sense of wonder about the natural world from these facts. And this goes into my writing. Knowledge like this can really bring out more wonder.

AL: *Zoomorphic* is now a place for animal-centric writing, and an example of a space for a truce between the exploitative, or at best ambivalent, dominant relationships that we humans have with other animals. What are your hopes for the publication going forward?

JR: You hope that somehow creating a community might contribute something, might change behavior, just a little. But I don't know. Is hope enough?

SR: I have to keep believing that *Zoomorphic* can have an impact. Poetry's a powerful tool because in addition to, or even often instead of, engaging the intellect, it aims to engage the heart. And once someone's made an emotional connection with a particular animal or animal-related issue, that connection's likely to be strong and enduring. It's hard to sustain hope in these challenging times, but I remain determined to continue developing *Zoomorphic*, equipped with the conviction that one of the best ways of celebrating and defending animals is by reconnecting our imaginations to them.

Resources for Writers

Here we have assembled a selected list of journals, magazines, and blogs dedicated to publishing animal-centric fiction and nonfiction. To view a more comprehensive and ongoing list of resources, visit www.ecolitbooks.com/literary-outlets-for-environmental-writing.

Journals & Magazines

Animal: A Beast of a Literary Magazine
www.animalliterarymagazine.com

Camas: The Nature of the West
www.camasmagazine.org

Ecozon@: European Journal of Literature, Culture and Environment
www.ecozona.eu

Ecotone
ecotonemagazine.org

Flyway
www.flywayjournal.org

ISLE: Interdisciplinary Studies in Literature and Environment
www.asle.org/research-write/isle-journal

Humanimalia
http://www.depauw.edu/site/humanimalia

Kudzu House Quarterly
www.kudzuhouse.org

Newfound
www.newfound.org

Orion magazine
www.orionmagazine.org

Saltfront: Studies in Human Habit(at)
www.saltfront.org

Sloth: A Journal of Emerging Voices in Human-Animal Studies
(for undergraduate students)
www.animalsandsociety.org/pages/sloth

Terrain.org
www.terrain.org

The Fourth River
www.thefourthriver.com

The Goose
http://scholars.wlu.ca/thegoose

The Hopper
www.hoppermag.org

Whole Terrain
www.wholeterrain.com

Zoomorphic
www.zoomorphic.net

Blogs

City Creatures Blog
Hosted by the Center for Humans and Nature
www.humansandnature.org/blog

EcoLit Books
Hosted by Ashland Creek Press
www.ecolitbooks.com

Eco-Fiction.com
www.eco-fiction.com

Contributors

Marybeth Holleman is the author of *The Heart of the Sound*, co-author of *Among Wolves*, and co-editor of *Crosscurrents North*. A Pushcart-Prize nominee, her essays, poems, and articles have appeared in dozens of journals, magazines, and anthologies, among them *Orion, Christian Science Monitor, Sierra, Literary Mama, North American Review, AQR,* and *The Future of Nature*, as well as on National Public Radio. Holleman has taught creative writing and women's studies at the University of Alaska and has written for nonprofits on environmental issues from polar bears to oil spills. A North Carolina transplant, she has lived in Alaska for more than twenty-five years.

Sangamithra Iyer is a writer and civil engineer. She is the author of *The Lines We Draw* (Hen Press), was a finalist for the 2016 Siskiyou Prize for New Environmental Literature, and is the editor of *Satya: The Long View* (2016). Sangu served as the assistant editor of *Satya* from 2004 to 2007, and as an associate for the public policy action tank Brighter Green. Her writing has been published by *n+1, Creative Nonfiction, Waging Nonviolence, Hippocampus Magazine, Local Knowledge,* Our

Hen House, and *VegNews*. Her essays have been anthologized in *Primate People: Saving Nonhuman Primates through Education, Advocacy and Sanctuary; Sister Species: Women, Animals and Social Justice*; and *Letters to a New Vegan*. She was a recipient of a Jerome Foundation literature travel grant and an artist residency at the Camargo Foundation. She lives in Queens, where she works on watershed protection and water supply infrastructure planning for New York City.

Lisa Johnson, PhD, JD, MFA, teaches and studies animal law and animals in society at the University of Puget Sound. She is also a fellow at the Oxford Centre for Animal Ethics. Her recent publications include "On the Suffering of Animals in Nature: Legal Barriers and the Moral Duty to Intervene" (2017) and "The Religion of Ethical Veganism" (2015), both published in the *Journal of Animal Ethics*; and *Power, Knowledge, Animals*, published by Palgrave-MacMillan (2012).

Hunter Liguore's life motto is "respect for differences." Her writing seeks to create a dialogue that promotes understanding our shared humanity as an alternative to discrimination and hate. She holds degrees in history and writing, and she teaches writing in New England. An award-winning writer, her work has appeared in over a hundred publications internationally, including *Spirituality & Health, Orion, Great Plains Quarterly*, and *Anthropology & Humanism*. She has several screenplays optioned, including *Everylife*, which is currently in pre-production. Her eco-fiction, teen novel, *Silent Winter*, is forthcoming and already being compared to *The Handmaid's Tale*. www.hunterliguore.org

Joanna Lilley is the author of the poetry collection *The Fleece Era* (Brick Books), which was nominated for the Fred Cogswell Award for Excellence in Poetry, and the short story collection *The Birthday Books* (Hagios Press). Her second poetry collection, *If There Were Roads*, was published in 2017 by Turnstone Press. Joanna emigrated from the UK to Yukon in Canada ten years ago. Find her at www.joannalilley.com.

Alex Lockwood is the author of *The Pig in Thin Air* (Lantern Books), an exploration of the place of the body in animal advocacy, as well as senior lecturer in journalism at the Centre for Research in Media and Cultural Studies, Sunderland University, UK. He has published widely on human-animal relations and is currently working on a series of novels concerned with human-animal conflict.

Rosemary Lombard is an animal behavior researcher/ herpetologist and has worked as a public school and university teacher, a naturalist on San Francisco Bay, and in the areas of water pollution and turtle cognition, among many others. A Northwest native, she has also lived in Idaho, the Midwest, New York, and California. She currently lives and works with fifteen turtle collaborators at an independent behavioral lab in Hillsboro, Oregon.

Beth Lyons is a former English literature teacher, award-winning poet, and traveler who now lives and writes in Portland, Oregon. She is the author of three fantasy novels and three science fiction novellas, all available via Amazon Kindle. In addition, she is a fiction editor, teaches workshops on editing and creative writing, and currently moderates an online writing forum.

Paula MacKay completed her MFA in Creative Writing at Pacific Lutheran University in 2015. For the past seventeen years, she has surveyed bears, wolverines, wolves, and other wildlife with her husband, Robert Long, with whom she co-edited *Noninvasive Survey Methods for Carnivores* (Island Press, 2008). Paula has written about animals and conservation for numerous organizations, scientific books and journals, and magazines. Her essay "My Sister's Shoes" was recently published in *Siblings: Our First Macrocosm*.

Midge Raymond is the author of the novel *My Last Continent* and the award-winning short-story collection *Forgetting English*. Her fiction, articles, and essays have appeared in *TriQuarterly, American Literary Review, Bellevue Literary Review*, the *Los Angeles Times* magazine, the *Chicago Tribune, Poets & Writers, LitHub, Zoomorphic, The Daily Beast, Daily Review* (Australia), *Barefoot Vegan, VegNews*, and many other publications.

Hannah Sandoval is a full-time freelance manuscript editor and ghostwriter and the founder of PurpleInkPen. She has a BA in English and is a proud member of the International Association of Professional Book Editors. Her novel *Arcamira* is the Best Fantasy Series winner of the 2017 Channillo Awards. Her Pembroke Welsh Corgi, Vanellope, embodies more sass than her owner could ever hope to.

Kipp Wessel's debut novel, *First, You Swallow the Moon*, a novel of heartbreak and wilderness, was a BookLife Prize in Fiction finalist and earned a *Writer's Digest* first-place award. His short stories have been published in a dozen commercial and literary magazines, and he's taught fiction writing at the

University of Montana (where he completed his MFA), the Loft Literary Center in Minneapolis, and regional community arts programs.

John Yunker writes plays, short stories, and novels focused on human/animal relationships. He is a co-founder of Ashland Creek Press, author of the novel *The Tourist Trail*, and editor of two fiction anthologies, *Among Animals* and *Among Animals 2*. His plays have been produced or staged at such venues as the Oregon Contemporary Theatre, the Source Festival, and the ATHE (Association for Theatre in Higher Education) conference. His teleplay *Sanctuary* was performed at the 2017 Compassion Arts Festival in New York, and his short stories have been published in *Phoebe, Qu, Flyway, Antennae*, and other journals.

About the Cover

Pictured on the cover is a quokka on Rottnest Island in Western Australia. Quokkas (*Setonix brachyurus*) are small marsupials that were mistakenly identified by early Europeans as small cats or rats. Today, the quokka is a protected species and a major tourist draw to Rottnest Island. And while a growing number of tourists arrive seeking selfies with these largely docile creatures, often going as far as to feed or pet them, fortunately a dedicated organization of volunteers is working to educate the public and to protect these amazing animals.

Also pictured on the cover is the keyboard of a 1938 Remington Remette portable typewriter.

Ashland Creek Press is a small, independent publisher of books for a better planet. Our mission is to publish a range of books that foster an appreciation for worlds outside our own, for nature and the animal kingdom, for the creative process, and for the ways in which we all connect. To keep up-to-date on new and forthcoming works, subscribe to our free newsletter by visiting www.AshlandCreekPress.com.

CPSIA information can be obtained
at www.ICGtesting.com
Printed in the USA
FFHW02n2250070818
47667603-51283FF

9 781618 220585